To Glenn

With all good wishes
To a fellow author and
lover of history. Hope you'll
learn more about the Niseis.
Your famous sensei
Edwin Nakasone
Aug 1999

THE NISEI SOLDIER

HISTORICAL ESSAYS
ON WORLD WAR II
AND THE KOREAN WAR

2nd Edition

By

Edwin M. Nakasone
Professor of History
Century College

Published by **J** - Press
4796 N. 126th St.
White Bear Lake, MN 55110

The Nisei Soldier
2nd edition
1st printing, April, 1999

Published by **J**-Press
4796 N. 126th St.
White Bear Lake, Mn. 55110

Printed and bound by Bang Printing, Brainerd, Minnesota

ISBN 0-9660111-5-5

Library of Congress Catalog Number: 98-75578

This book is dedicated to

my wife, Mary

my sons, John and Paul

my grand children, Jacob, Mariko, Natalie and Sarah *& Daniel*

**May they continue to remember
and reflect upon their proud heritage**

CONTENTS

AUTHOR'S FOREWORD
TO THE 2ND EDITION

In less than a year the twentieth century will close and the dawning of the twenty first century will be upon us. If one were to assess the most significant event, the one that impacted the whole world and changed our life styles immeasurably, most, I feel, will mention or choose World War II, 1937-1945. This was the event that affected our great grandparents, our grand parents, our parents, the children, you, me and the coming generations.

A full understanding of this most significant event requires that we attempt to examine it from as many perspectives as possible. One of these perspectives, an often neglected one, is that of the Japanese American citizens who, though they participated in the war to defend their country as outstanding soldiers, were also persecuted by their government and distrusted by other Americans.

Terms often used to describe Japanese Americans are "Nisei" (children born to the immigrant Issei parents) and "AJA"—Americans of Japanese ancestry. At the outbreak of World War II, there were approximately 160,000 Japanese-Americans in Hawaii, and 126,000 on the mainland, 113,000 of whom were residing on the west coast. As a Nisei himself, this author lived through WWII, participated in the U.S. military occupation of Japan, and has specialized in teaching the historical events, trauma, and consequences of the great second world war. Therefore, I feel especially qualified to relate not only the historical events themselves, but also to focus on the Japanese American perspective on these events—as well as to attempt to present the Japanese side.

The book is organized as a series of essays I have written over the years. This second edition of *The Nisei Soldier* has added seven more essays to the original five in the first edition. These new essays continue the theme of providing a synoptic view of World War II, especially from the

Japanese-American perspective. As with the first edition, the essays have not been written with any particular connection to one another. The format I have used to organize the book simply places the papers in the order in which they were written. The reader should understand, therefore, that there is a good deal of moving back and forth in time. Nevertheless, the chronology of the events of the war as herein described should be fairly evident. Each of the essays is introduced by the author's reflections of its relevance and connection to World War II and the Korean war.

In the essay "Pearl Harbor Remembered," this author, who was an eyewitness of the attack on that fateful day of December 7, 1941, describes the thinking, planning, training, and the attack itself and the results, as carried out by the Imperial Japanese Navy.

"Go For Broke" extols the virtues of the young Nisei of the 40's—the suspect Japanese Americans—the gallant, patriotic children of immigrant Japanese parents who volunteered to show all Americans their true love of America and all she stood for. Their unit, the 442nd Regimental Combat Team, became the most decorated unit of the armed forces of the United States.

"America's Secret Warriors" is the fascinating story of how the Nisei linguists were so effective as interpreters, translators, interrogators, and of how they analyzed the entire Japanese language, culture and communication systems so that U.S. military leaders acknowledged, afterward, that they probably saved millions of lives and shortened the war by two years.

"Kamikaze" is the story of how Japan was able to assemble a suicidal last ditch effort to save her imperial shores from the expected invasion of the "American monsters." The author examines the psychological and emotional status of Japan's young volunteers, their hurried training and their fiery deaths.

The essay, "Japan in War and Peace—Yesterday's Enemy Is

Today's Friend"—is the result of the author interviewing Japanese war veterans—a revealing look at how the veterans of Japan looked upon the war.

The essay "Chiune (Sempo) Sugihara: Japan's Oskar Schindler," is the story of one Japanese citizen who refused to obey the orders of his superiors and issued thousands of visas to Jews, thus allowing them to escape the death camps of the Nazis.

The article on the Japanese Peruvians (which includes other Japanese Latin Americans) illustrates the sad tale of over 2,000 WWII victims who were kidnapped or taken forcibly from their homes and removed to U.S. concentration camps.

The essay on the experiences and treatment of Mrs. Iva Toguri D'Aquino, a stranded Nisei woman, who was arrested, tried, and vilified by our media and government as "Tokyo Rose" shows the great animosity toward Japanese American citizens, even after many of them had fought valiantly for their adopted homeland. Her story is truly the antithesis of what we Americans hold dearly—fair play. Her constitutional rights were negated as she was victimized by our post-war government's desire to garner a scapegoat.

The essay entitled "Balloon Bombing" portrays Japan's desperation, bordering on despair, as evidenced by her military's attempt to bomb America via giant paper balloons.

The essay by Spady Koyama, a WWII and Korean War veteran, contributes enormously to the theme of human kindness and the oft-repeated Japanese saying "yesterday's enemy is today's friend." Spady's work as an interrogator of Japanese POWs earned him the love, admiration and undying respect of a Japanese POW, manifested to him long after the war was over.

The essay entitled "Little Switch" takes the reader to the Korean War and tells how one Nisei soldier struggled valiantly against North Korean brutality in their POW camps. Susumu (Sus) Shinagawa suffered through 34 months of cruel captivity. His story will evoke anger, sorrow, and hatred; yet, finally, one must respect, admire and come to revere and salute the courage and patriotism of this brave Nisei soldier.

In essence, then, this book is the story of the remarkable Japanese American citizens, and of their little known participation in and experience of the events of World War II. There can be little doubt that the participation of Japanese American citizens in World War II was one of the decisive factors in bringing the war to an end.

I wish to express my gratitude to all those who aided me in the writing of this book: those who reviewed the book; my students who evaluated the book from a student's perspective; my colleague and editor, Professor Sidney Jackson, who had the unenviable task of editing and suggesting corrections; and, of course, to my wife and family who encouraged me on this writing venture. To all of these, I say "thank you." Also, a rejoinder: there may be errors, and for those, I, as the author, take full responsibility.

The author hopes that these essays will aid the reader in knowing important facets of the most significant event of the twentieth century, World War II. I hope, also, that these papers and articles will enrich the reader by showing important facets of World War II and the Korean War as viewed from a Japanese American's perspective. Hopefully, readers will learn the opposing viewpoints of the Japanese, too.

Edwin M. Nakasone
Professor of History
Century College,
March, 1999

CHAPTER ONE

PEARL HARBOR REMEMBERED

Introduction

In assessing Japan's surprise attack on Pearl Harbor one must keep in mind her samurai heritage and her pre-World War II moves into Asia. By summer and fall of 1941, Japan had occupied Taiwan, Korea, Manchuria, China, and French Indochina, and had signed a friendship treaty with Thailand. The aggressive moves into China and French Indochina created an international crisis that resulted in a U.S. economic blockade, and the freezing of all Japanese financial accounts in the United States. This precipitated the Hull-Nomura/Kurusu talks. President Roosevelt had instructed Secretary of State Cordell Hull to demand that all Japanese troops be removed from China and Indochina before negotiations could begin. A stalemate ensued since General Tojo's cabinet could not withdraw without losing face.

Yamamoto's Planning and Training Staff

The Imperial Japanese Navy (IJN) knew that Japan's projected hegemony in Asia could not proceed unless the U.S. Pacific Fleet was eliminated at Pearl Harbor. Eleven months prior to the attack at Pearl Harbor, Japan's Chief of the Combined Fleet Admiral Isoroku Yamamoto, had formulated a daring plan to bomb Pearl Harbor, home of the U.S. Pacific Fleet. He called in Vice Admiral Takejiro Onishi[1] and told the surprised Onishi of his decision, whereupon

Admiral Isoroku Yamamoto, architect of the Pearl Harbor attack (U.S. Navy Archives photo).

Onishi recommended as Staff Planning Officer, Commander Minoru Genda. Genda, a young, brilliant naval flying officer, as equally surprised as Onishi when informed by Yamamoto of the Pearl Harbor decision, immediately began his research and planning. Genda recommended Commander Fuchida to be the chief air officer in charge of training and in leading the attacking pilots into Pearl Harbor.[2] Genda needed the latest intelligence concerning all elements of Pearl Harbor and the island's defenses. At this juncture one must introduce Japan's most accomplished spy of WWII—Ensign Takeo Yoshikawa, alias Tadashi Morimura.[3]

Vice Admiral Chuichi Nagumo, Pearl Harbor attack commander (U.S. Navy Archives photo).

Master Spy Takeo Yoshikawa

On 27 March 1941, Yoshikawa arrived in Honolulu and he soon made the Japanese Consulate on Honolulu's Nuuanu Avenue the espionage center for Operation Z (the Imperial Japanese Navy's Pearl Harbor operation). Only Consul General Nagao Kita knew Yoshikawa's real mission as he introduced him to all as "Tadashi Morimura." Yoshikawa's mission was to ferret out

Master spy Takeo Yoshikawa, 1969 (photo courtesy of Parade magazine)

all the information needed by Genda's planning section, so he surprised all the other clerks with his unusual work schedule: in at ll00 hours and out by 1300 hours. All wondered what he was doing during his f r e q u e n t absences.[4]

Yoshikawa was soon hard at work on his intelligence mission. Initially, he circled the island by car to locate all airbases and airfields. Then he took frequent air flights over Oahu from Honolulu's John Rogers Airport, pinpointing all ships by size and shape, storing the info in his memory bank—he never took notes. Subsequently, he would slip into the consul headquarters and send the info to naval headquarters in Tokyo by code.

He even presented himself as a Filipino to the manager of the Pearl Harbor Officers Club, and blurted out "Me Filipino, me want job." The manager asked, "Can you bartend? No, no, never mind, wipe off the tables and clean up the ash trays." As Yoshikawa worked around the tables he noted, again in his mind, how American officers after one drink or more tended to discuss all the latest info—what ships came in, what ships went out. The info gained was sent as the latest intelligence from Hawaii.

The Pearl Harbor attack plan called for five midget submarines to infiltrate and enter the harbor prior to the attack, and during the attack to torpedo the capital ships, preferably aircraft carriers. Genda needed to know the depth and composition of the channel leading into the harbor. Again, Yoshikawa provided this vital intelligence by posing as a local fisherman. He cast fishing lines from the shore to determine the approximate depth and the exact consistency of the channel bottom. He found that the channel was deep enough and that the bottom would permit safe passage of the midget submarines to proceed into Pearl Harbor.

Yoshikawa often posed as a hard drinking Japanese and frequented a Japanese inn—a tea house that was then located in Aiea Heights overlooking Pearl Harbor. Soon he gained the confidence of the tea house owner as he feigned drunken stupor—"it was better to have Yoshikawa sleep off his drunk rather than be a menace on the streets and highways," the owner rationalized. Yoshikawa, left in the inn by himself, would awaken early in the morning and with binoculars continue to survey the type of ships and their locations in the harbor. So, Yamamoto's intelligence concerning the U.S. Pacific Fleet was amazingly complete and up to date, thanks to Japan's master spy, Takeo Yoshikawa.

Commanders Fuchida and Genda

Commander Fuchida was recommended to be the flight leader and trainer of all the attacking pilots by Commander Genda and duly approved by Rear Admiral Ryunosuke Kusaka, executive to the flotilla commander, Vice Admiral Chuichi Nagumo. They selected some 400 of the navy's best pilots and they, without any inkling as to the ultimate objective, were trained diligently by Fuchida. They trained in the Inland Sea ports of Kure, Saeki, and in Kyushu's Kagoshima Bay.[5]

Fuchida, who had over 5,000 hours of combat flying in China, had the flyers train in low and high altitude bombing, dog fighting, and mastering the low flying short torpedo runs. Aerial torpedoes were the "babies" of Genda—he wanted to guarantee sinking the capital ships in the harbor. Yet, aerial torpedoes involved great intricacies in a crowded, shallow basin such as Pearl Harbor.[6] The aerial torpedo, when dropped from the plane, plunged to a depth of 80 to 110 feet before rising to a level plane and thrusting forward. Genda discovered that when the Royal Air Force sank the Italian fleet in shallow Taranto Bay (60 feet depth) it had installed extra fins on their torpedoes. Genda went one better than the English and installed wooden fins and wooden stabilizers (at end of torpedo) which would sheer off as the torpedoes entered the water. The fins and stabilizers prevented the deep dive of the torpedoes. The torpedoes would submerge only to about 30 feet. Success!

Also, pilots had to be proficient in lining their planes toward the target for the torpedo run was no longer than one half mile, some runs being even shorter. Bomber pilots were trained to hold on to their bombing runs no matter the antiaircraft fire. Their light planes were hauling 1,000 and 2,000 pound bombs developed from armor piercing artillery shells. Genda and Fuchida wanted to facilitate the bombs going through the main decks to explode inside the ships.[7] Fighter pilots were trained to patrol above the bombers and torpedo planes at the 10,000 to 15,000 foot level, keeping alert to engage any defending planes over the assigned target areas.

The Pearl Harbor Attack

With negotiations at a standstill, Admiral Yamamoto decided to act. On 10 through 18 November, 1941, singly, thirty one ships sailed out of Kure, out of the Inland Sea, and headed north to Tankan Bay in the Kurile Islands. Absolute secrecy prevailed. All those aboard were ordered to wear summer uniforms. "Ah so!" they said, "we're on our way to the Philippines." Soon as they cleared Japan and headed north, they put on their winter uniforms and they exclaimed, "Ah ha, It's not the Philippines, but Alaska, yes Alaska!" Then too, the regular radio operators and telegraphers were ordered mariners Sakamaki and his crew member, Kioshi Inagaki, took a hot bath aboard their carrier sub, the I-24, then perfumed themselves with cologne, thus, symbolizing their impending kamikaze sub attack to the short lived beautiful cherry blossoms. Sakamaki, aboard his midget sub, cast off from his mother sub but soon found that he was headed west, towards Japan, instead of heading for the entry way of Pearl Harbor. Something was, as he related later, "no working." He ordered Inagaki to carry the 20 pound ballasts from the rear of the sub to the bow. With the sub balanced off, he turned the craft around and headed for the harbor. "CRASH!" Within minutes Sakamaki had piloted the sub onto submerged reefs and his bow was now above water. Once more he ordered crew member Inagaki to go to the front and transfer the heavy ballasts to the stern. Then Sakamaki heavily gunned and gunned the throttle. Result, the sub's electric batteries exploded spraying them in noxious chemical fumes that caused both to gag and fall unconscious.

Truly, Sakamaki was like cartoonist Al Capp's proverbial hard luck and jinxed character, Joe B*t#f@s!k. The sub floated helplessly around Diamond Head, Hanauma Bay, Oahu's southeast point of Makapuu, and finally came to rest on coral reefs off Bellows Airfield. The following day Inagaki got up before Sakamaki and attempted to swim to shore—he drowned. Sakamaki, not knowing where Inagaki had disappeared to, dove into the waters and barely dragged himself

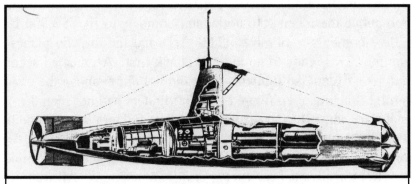

A Japanese midget submarine like the one piloted by Ensign Sakamaki (U.S. Navy Archives drawing).

on to shore where he was immediately captured by a national guard soldier. Sakamaki thus became our nation's POW Number One.[13]

Sunday Morning 7 December, 1941

By 0630 hours the first wave, led by Commander Fuchida, was roaring off the flight decks of the main carrier Akagi. These planes were soon joined by those winging off from the other five carriers, *Hiryu, Kaga, Shokaku, Zuikaku* and *Soryu*. By 0830 hours the second wave was winging their way to Pearl Harbor. All in all, 353 planes were dispatched from a point 230 miles north of Oahu.[14] Other than the flight leaders, pilots were without radios and were instructed to head towards the northern island of Niihau after the raid and follow the leaders toward their waiting carriers.

As Fuchida and the lead planes reached Pearl Harbor, Fuchida radioed back to the Akagi: "*Tora, Tora, Tora!*" ("We have achieved complete surprise!"). Miraculously, this radio message was even received by naval headquarters in Tokyo. According to the pilots interviewed, if surprise had been achieved, Fuchida would signal with one signal flare that he would shoot in the air. This called for the torpedo planes to go in first and release their torpedoes. If surprise had been compromised then two flares would be fired and all planes would commence with their attacks simultaneously. Fuchida fired the one flare and he coolly waited to see if the fighters would climb above the others, the horizontal bombers to fly at 3,500 feet, the dive bombers to climb to 12,000 feet and the torpedo planes to skim the waves ready to go into the attack first. All reacted according to plan except the fighters—they did not climb above the others. Horrors! Fuchida then figured that the fighters had not seen the one signal flare and fired the second flare. The fighters then responded, but the others, thinking that the second flare had now been fired zoomed to the attack simultaneously. The fighters and dive bombers went after the airfields and anti-aircraft gun positions. All went well despite the snafu and the fighters and dive bombers went after the airfields and antiaircraft guns and the torpedo planes came in from the

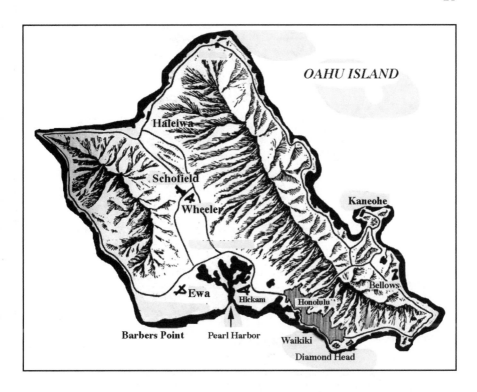

southeast to release their torpedoes against the battleships.[15]

The first bomb went off at 0755. The attack on Pearl Harbor had commenced. Aerial torpedoes were launched against all ships on battleship row. All outboard battleships, *Oklahoma*, *West Virginia*, *California*, *Nevada* and the *Utah* (it was used as a target ship and was located on the north side of Ford Island) were attacked. The *Oklahoma* rolled over, bottom side up, while the *Utah* sank with one side resting in the muck of Ford Island.

Meanwhile, the *Nevada's* crew was able to crank up two of its four boilers and, avoiding the torpedoes, slowly maneuvered toward the entrance channel, hoping to escape from the disastrous harbor site. As she neared the entrance, the attacking planes veered towards her with the intent to sink the ship in the channel and thus close off Pearl Harbor. Lieutenant Commander Francis Thomas, senior officer on board that morning, realizing the obvious situation, ordered the engines to be cut and he rammed the huge battleship into Hospital

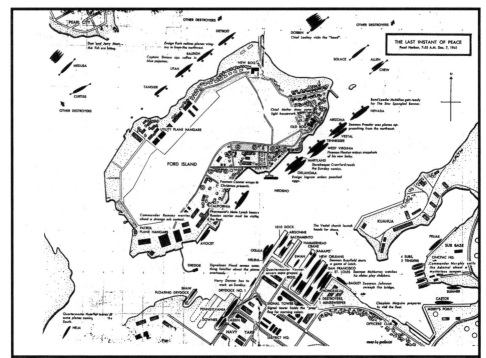

Map of Pearl Harbor with location of U.S. Navy vessels at 7.55 AM, Dec. 7, 1941, the time of the Japanese attack. (U.S. Navy archives).

Point near the entrance channel.[16]

The *Arizona*, with the small repair ship *Vestal* on the outboard, still suffered two torpedo hits. The horizontal bombers, led by Commander Fuchida, now went for the inboard *Arizona*. Steel began raining down on the huge ship. Number 4 and number 6 gun turrets were hit but the *coup de gras'* was a 2,000 pound artillery gun shell designed as a penetration bomb—it crashed alongside number 2 turret through the forecastle and with a gigantic roar set off the forward magazines. The *Arizona* settled to the shallow bottom in nine minutes. Over 1,100 men were entombed in the ship.[17] One of Fuchida's men recalled seeing the huge fireball and yelled, "*atarimashita!*" ("a hit!").

Fuchida then circled the combat area and headed north slowly, making a deliberate zigzagging movement to allow any "lost" pilot to follow the path back to the carriers. Landing on the *Akagi*, Fuchida quickly left the plane in the hands of the deck crew and dashed to the bridge. He blurted out to Admiral Nagumo, "Where's the third wave? Where's the third wave?"

Nagumo responded, "Commander Fuchida, have we hit all the assigned targets?" "Yes sir," answered Fuchida. "Then we go home." Nagumo, a battleship expert, was deathly afraid of losing any of his six carriers. Japan had but eight carriers in its entire naval force at that time. Fuchida, with tears in his eyes, gulped down his tremendous disappointment, saluted the commander, and withdrew from the bridge.

What were the results of this brazen surprise attack? Of 92 ships then in the harbor, eighteen capital ships had been sunk or heavily damaged: *Arizona, Oklahoma, Utah, Oglala, Cassin,* and *Downes* were lost. *West Virginia, California, Tennessee, Maryland, Nevada, Pennsylvania, Helena, Honolulu, Raleigh* and *Shaw* were heavily damaged. We lost 188 planes (96 army, 92 navy) as the Japanese fighters and bombers raided each air base except the well

Nine of the ten submarine crewmen who died in the Pearl Harbor attack (U.S. Navy Archives photo).

hidden small fighter strip at Haleiwa, and 159 planes were damaged. Our personnel losses came to 2,403 killed (over 1,100 on the *Arizona*) and 1,178 wounded.[18]

Japanese losses were comparatively light with 29 planes lost, one submarine, five midget submarines, 55 airmen, nine midget submariners, and an unknown number on the submarine.[19]

Fuchida, was questioned after the war, "Why weren't the unprotected fuel tanks, the submarine base and the repair facilities bombed?" He answered, "They were not part of the main attack plans and I had hoped to take them out with a third wave. We wanted to avoid obscuring the main targets (ships) with black smoke if the tanks had been hit. Also, we wanted to take aerial photos to evaluate the results."

Niihau Island Incident: The Nishikaichi Story

A final episode to reflect upon is the Niihau Island incident. Recall that all pilots were to fly north towards the waiting carriers and if unable to do so, they were to head towards Niihau island and attempt to land on this "uninhabited" island.[20] Then, by waiting off the northwest coast of Niihau they would be rescued by submarines. Naval Airman 1st Class Shigenori Nishikaichi, pilot of the single seater A6M Zero fighter, had flown off the deck of the carrier *Hiryu* at 0730. He was in the second wave with eight other fighters escorting eight high level bombers. By 0835 hours they were bombing and strafing Kaneohe Naval Air Station, then they attacked Bellows Airfield, a stone's throw away. By 0945 their group was about to return when nine American P-36 fighter planes swooped down on the zeroes. A dog fight ensued and Nishikaichi was able to shoot down one plane. But, in the melee, his plane suffered six bullet hits, one puncturing the gas line. Sputtering and falling behind the others he had to seek a landing place. Niihau loomed ahead. Circling the small (19 x 8 miles) island once, he picked out a likely spot and crash-landed in the plowed field. Nishikaichi was knocked unconscious.

The natives were dumfounded. Having no radio or telephone

they were completely unaware of the Pearl Harbor attack. Several of the men cautiously approached the plane and pulled out the unconscious pilot, took his pistol, maps and charts, and secured him in one of their cottages. When Nishikaichi awakened he peered out the window and spotted a Japanese man walking by. He hollered, "*Anone, anone, Nihonjin des ka?*" ("Hello, Hello, are you Japanese?"). The Japanese man, a Mr. Harada, was the bookkeeper for the Robinson family. He hurried over and responded, "Yes, I am, but what are you doing here?"

Nishikaichi informed Harada of the attack and demanded his help in recovering the pistol, maps and charts, so that he could be rescued by the submarines. Also, he did not want the maps and charts to fall into the hands of the U.S. military to avoid U.S. planes attacking Japan's fleet. Harada released the pilot and they both began searching the native Hawaiians' homes. Harada was able to obtain a pistol and a shotgun that had been hidden in one of the warehouses. Try as they might they could not find the maps and charts. The days and nights were slipping by, Nishikaichi getting more and more desperate as the days passed. By Saturday, 13 December, frantic Niihauans had rowed across the 20 mile channel to Kauai to inform authorities of the rampaging Japanese pilot. They had even lighted giant bonfires facing Kauai to attempt signaling Kauai.

Meanwhile Nishikaichi, aided by Harada, continued terrorizing the natives with their weapons.[21] They bullied and searched for the pistol and papers. Soon they came to the home of Benjamin and Ella Kanahele. Now Ben was a large Hawaiian rancher standing 6'2" and weighing over 200 pounds. The pilot faced Ben and demanded "Give me papers! Give me papers!" Ben, not knowing what he was referring to, strode towards Nishikaichi. Nishikaichi, fearful and desperate, shot Ben three times. Though seriously wounded, Ben grabbed the pilot as he would one of his sheep, lifted the man and hurled him against the stone wall. Then Ella bashed in Nishikaichi's head even as Ben slashed the pilot's throat. Harada, seeing all this, panicked. He jammed the shotgun into his stomach and committed suicide.[22]

Nishikaichi was later posthumously honored by the Japanese

Imperial Navy with an advancement in rank to ensign.

Epilogue

Historian Samuel Eliot Morison often referred to the Pearl Harbor attack as the greatest offensive "blunder" made by the Imperial Japanese Navy.[23] Why? Morison's charge resulted from three different aspects of the attack. First, the pilots failed to bomb the fuel tanks located so openly around the harbor. Second, the submarine pens were not attacked. Third, Pearl Harbor's repair shops and facilities were not destroyed. Fuchida explained in later interviews that their planning was based on an attack that was extremely risky at best, and so only prime targets were designated, those being aircraft carriers, battleships, and other larger ships, such as cruisers. If the fuel tanks were to be bombed the constricted harbor would be completely covered in black smoke thereby voiding accurate bomb and aerial torpedo drops. If they were to have been bombed after the main raid the smoke would have prevented aerial photos to give the Japanese an accurate appraisal of the damage inflicted. Fuchida explained that the submarine pens were secluded and difficult to hit. Rather, their goal was to hit the "open" ships—hit hard and get out of there. The repair facilities were not even considered, according to Commander Fuchida.

It was Admiral Morison's contention that the attack was a tactical and psychological blunder because ships sunk were resurfaced, repaired and sent out to battle once more because of the shallow depth of Pearl Harbor. Psychologically, it bound the United States into a unified nation with the call to "Remember Pearl Harbor!" The undamaged fuel tanks were immediately fueling the submarines, planes, and surface ships. Within a matter of weeks we attacked the Japanese at the Caroline and Marshall Islands and by April, 1942, the famous Doolittle Raids were conducted over Tokyo and other Japanese cities. Morison's arguments are convincing when viewed from the results of the Pacific naval battles and from the original Imperial naval strategy. The strategy was to inveigle the American

Pacific Fleet out of Pearl Harbor and in several decisive battles on the high seas, with torpedoes, shelling and aerial bombings, sink forever the American fleet. This did not occur and Pearl Harbor served to be the binding strength of the American people, her navy and the rest of the American armed forces. In reality the attack on Pearl Harbor did "awaken the sleeping giant" that Admiral Isoroku Yamamoto had warned the Japanese about.

Notes

1. Vice Admiral Ohnishi was the originator of the Kamikaze tactic which began their suicidal attacks beginning October, 1944.

2. Commander Fuchida was one of the most brilliant flyers in the IJN (Imperial Japanese Navy) and had over 5,000 combat flying hours already.

3. Edwin T. Layton, p. 111.

4. Yoshikawa had failed to qualify as a naval pilot due to illness. He was assigned to naval intelligence where he received extensive training in identifying Allied ships, planes, and weaponry.

5. Kagoshima Bay with its Sakurajima Island resembled Pearl Harbor with its Ford Island.

6 The average depth of Pearl Harbor was 44 to 45 feet.

7. BB *Arizona's* deck was pierced and the 2000# bomb exploded in the arsenal hold.

8. Refueling continued until 6 December and then the tankers were released to return to Japan (Pearl Harbor Tapes, "The Storm Unleashed").

9. Lord, p. 22.

10. Their underwear was to be white since Japan believed white to be

the symbol of purity.

11. This was the traditional type of folding for special occasions, ala origami, a well known method of Japanese paper folding.

12. Midget subs were 80 feet long, six feet in diameter at their widest point and displaced 46 tons. Each boat carried two 18-inch torpedoes and was controlled by a two-man crew. It was powered by small electric batteries with top speed at 23 knots on the surface, 19 knots submerged (Cohen, p.77).

13. Sakamaki was captured by a Hawaii National Guardsman at Bellows Airfield beach, then transferred to a temporary holding camp at Sand Island, and subsequently sent to Camp McCoy, Wisconsin, where he was imprisoned for two years. He spent the rest of the war in POW camps located in Texas and Tennessee.

14. The 353 planes were in two waves and dependent on the type of plane (torpedo, bomber, fighter) they had been assigned definite targets. Each carrier's planes were given specific targets and were also to hit targets of opportunity if their primary targets were destroyed or unavailable. They were also instructed to head towards the northerly island of Niihau, and to crash land near an islet off shore from Niihau where they would have mother subs around to rescue them. Except for the squadron commander's planes, the pilots did not have access to plane radios.

15. Lord, audio tapes.

16. Lord, p. 136.

17. Lord, p. 97.

18. Prange, p. 513.

19. Prange, p. 513.

20. Niihau has been referred to as the "forbidden" island by many local Hawaiians because it was a private island owned since the 1860's by the Robinson family. They had purchased the island from King Kamehameha IV for $10,000 in gold. It was always kept in the

Hawaiian life style of the 1880's with no newspapers, radio, telephone, telegraph or other signal equipment. It was completely isolated. It was an island where Hawaiian was the spoken language and only the native Niihau-acclimated Hawaiians were allowed to live there. The only exceptions at that time were three Japanese persons who were the bookkeeper/storekeeper married couple, and the personal gardener/handyman of Mr Aylmer Robinson, who lived on the neighboring island of Kauai.

21. 182 Hawaiians were registered for Niihau in the 1940 census.

22. A short but excellent narrative of the whole incident is captured in Allan Beekman, *The Niihau Incident*, 1982 (See bibliography).

23. Captain Roger Pineau's interview with Admiral Sadatoshi Tomioka, in *The Pearl Harbor Tapes*, "The Storm Unleashed," 1992.

Selected Bibliography

Books:

Agawa, Hiroyuki, *The Reluctant Admiral: Yamamoto And The Imperial Japanese Navy* (New York, NY: Harper and Row, 1979).

Bergamini, David, *Japan's Imperial Conspiracy* (New York, NY: William Morrow, 1971).

Butow, Robert J.C., *Tojo And The Coming Of The War* (Princeton, NJ: Princeton University Press, 1961).

Clark, Blake, *Remember Pearl Harbor* (New York, NY: Modern Age Books, 1942).

Cohen, Stan, *East Wind Rain: A Pictorial History Of The Pearl Harbor Attack* (Missoula, MT: Pictorial Histories Publishing Co., 1989).

Costello, John, *The Pacific War* (New York, NY: Rawson and Wade, 1981).

Farago, Ladislas, *The Broken Seal: Operation Magic And The Pearl Harbor Disaster* (New York, NY: Random House, 1967).

Feis, Herbert, *The Road To Pearl Harbor* (Princeton, NJ: Princeton University Press, 1950).

Fuchida, Mitsuo, Masatake Okumiya, Translated by. Masataka Chihaya, *Midway :The Battle That Doomed Japan*, Clarke H. Kawakami and Roger Pineau eds. (Annapolis, MD: U.S. Naval Institute Press, 1955).

Ienaga, Saburo, *The Pacific War 1931-1945* (New York, NY: Pantheon Books, 1968).

Jablonski, Edward, *Flying Fortress* (Garden City, NY, Doubleday, 1965).

Layton, Edwin T., *And I Was There* (New York, NY: Wm. Morrow & Co., 1985).

Lord, Walter, *Day Of Infamy* (New York, NY: Holt Rinehart & Co., 1957).

Morison, Samuel Eliot, *Coral Sea, Midway And Submarine Actions, May 1942-August 1942* (Boston, MA: Little Brown & Co., 1949).

_____, *The Rising Sun In The Pacific* (Boston, MA: Little Brown & Co., 1948).

Okumiya, Masatake, and Jiro Horikoshi, with Martin Caidin, *Zero!* (New York, NY: E. P. Dutton, 1956).

Sakai, Saburo, with Fred Saito and Martin Caidin, *Samurai* (Garden City, NY: Nelson Doubleday, Inc., 1957).

Sakamaki, Kazuo, *I Attacked Pearl Harbor* (New York, NY: Association Press, 1949).

Sheehan, Ed., *Days Of '41* (Honolulu, HI: Kapa Associates,1977).

Slackman, Michael, *Remembering Pearl Harbor:The Story Of The USS Arizona Memorial* (Honolulu, HI: Arizona Memorial Association, 1987).

Terasaki, Gwen, *Bridge To The Sun* (Chapel Hill, NC: University of North Carolina Press, 1970).

Zich, Arthur, *The Rising Sun WWII* (Alexandria, VA: Time-Life Books, Inc., 1977).

Toland, John, *The Rising Sun: The Decline And Fall Of The Japanese Empire*, 1936-1945 (New York, NY: Random House, 1970).

Wilmott, H.P., *Pearl Harbor* (New York, NY: Gallery Books, 1981).

Wohlsetter, Roberta, *Pearl Harbor Warning And Decision* (Stanford, CA: Stanford University Press, 1962).

Magazines, Newspapers, Pamphlets

"World War II," *The American Legion*, Commemorative Issue, Sept., 1991.

"World War II," *Profile*, Commemorative Issue, Nov., 1993.

Honolulu Star-Bulletin, 1st Extra, Vol. XIVIII, No. 15359, 7 Dec., 1941.

Pacific Citizen, Vol. 73, No. 26, 24-31 Dec., 1971.

Pacific Stars And Stripes, Vol. 46, No. 334, 1 Dec., 1991.

"*After The Battle, Pearl Harbor Then And Now*," No. 38, 1982.

"*The Day Of Infamy*," Hofstra University Museum, 50th Anniversary of the Bombing of Pearl Harbor, 1 Dec., 1991 - 20 Jan., 1992.

Hudson, Robert S., *Sunrise Sunset* (Honolulu, Hawaii, 1986).

Lott, Arnold S., and Robert F. Sumrall, *Pearl Harbor Attack*, (Honolulu, HI: Fleet Reserve Association, 1977).

World War II, WWII 50th Anniversary Issue, (Leesburg, VA: Empire Press, November 1991).

Audiovisual Media Sources

Lord, Walter, "The Storm Unleashed," (audio tapes) Vols. I and II, 1992 (Arizona Memorial Museum Association, #1 Arizona Place, Honolulu, HI 96813, Phone (808) 868-1234. These are twenty six excellent audio tapes recorded during the 50th anniversary celebration held at Pearl Harbor. The tapes include many of the raid participants, both American and Japanese, as well as the civilians caught in the attack.

"Japanese Pilots Interview," Parts I and II, 1986, author's private collection.
"World War II With Walter Cronkite," (Terre Haute, IN: Columbia House Video Library, P.O. Box 1112, Dept. CTR).

Nakasone, Edwin M., "Pearl Harbor Remembered," videocassette, 1990.

CHAPTER TWO

GO FOR BROKE: THE NISEI 442nd REGIMENTAL COMBAT TEAM

Introduction

The purpose of this essay is to familiarize the reader with the United States Army's most decorated unit, the 442nd Regimental Combat Team, which included the famed 100th Infantry Battalion. It will trace the unit from its WWII beginnings to the present and emphasize the rich human legacy left by this courageous unit. In essence, this is the story of a remarkable people, the Japanese Americans. Terms often used to describe Japanese Americans are Nisei (children born to the immigrant Issei parents) and AJA—Americans of Japanese ancestry. At the outbreak of World War II, those of Japanese ancestry numbered approximately 160,000 in Hawaii, and 126,000 on the mainland, 113,000 of whom were residing on the west coast.[1]

With the advent of conscription in 1940, and by December 7, 1941, the day of the bombing of Pearl Harbor in Hawaii, over 1,400 Nisei had been drafted in Hawaii. After basic training at Schofield Barracks they were assigned to the already federalized 298th and 299th Infantry Regiments of the Hawaii National Guard. When the national guard was federalized, the Territory of Hawaii organized a Territorial Guard, in which over 300 Niseis, primarily University of

Hawaii ROTC (Reserve Officer Training Corps) cadets, had been recruited. (More about them later.)

Pearl Harbor and Its Immediate Impact

The attack on Pearl Harbor brought all Issei and Nisei under suspicion. Some authorities even charged them with espionage and sabotage.[2] Secretary of the Navy Frank Knox, for example, demanded that all ethnic Japanese be transported to the mainland or be incarcerated on one island, Molokai. Fortunately, cooler heads prevailed,

The Honolulu Star-Bulletin headlines the outbreak of World War II.

those being Hawaii Army commander, General Delos C. Emmons, FBI chief Robert L. Shivers, and Army G-2 (Military Intelligence) Colonel Kendall J. Fielder.[3] Nevertheless, while they were not incarcerated, those 300 Nisei members of the Hawaii Territorial Guard were brusquely called in, their weapons taken, were discharged and sent home. They were not to be trusted. Other Asians—Chinese, Koreans, Filipinos, Hawaiians and part Hawaiians—were kept in the Territorial Guard, but not those of Japanese ancestry. Racism apparently had triumphed. This was a crushing blow to these Niseis! Yet, these young men, undaunted, volunteered their labor services to the army, sans pay, as the "Varsity Victory Volunteers."[4]

The other 1,400 Nisei soldiers who had already been drafted into the regular army posed a special problem for the top military leaders since many commanders had no faith nor trust in them. Almost certainly, many of these commanders felt that the draftee's Japanese facial and physical features would not allow them to serve in the Pacific against the Japanese. These Nisei soldiers were thus pulled out of the 298th and 299th, based on their ethnicity, and were temporarily assigned as a provisional battalion. Many of these Nisei felt that their battalion would be a labor unit, mopping up after the white troops. Discontent, low morale, and anxiety visited the battalion members. They wanted to be combat soldiers. They wanted to prove to all that they could be trusted, that their country was America and that they were all Americans, not Japanese. It was at this juncture that General Emmons requested the War Department to send the Nisei soldiers to the mainland for training as infantry soldiers.[5] The Niseis were sent to the mainland in June 1942 and assigned to the 100th Infantry Battalion. They began training at Camp McCoy, Wisconsin.

Meanwhile, conscription of Japanese Americans had been halted and Niseis eligible for the draft were classified 4C, "Undesirable," another crushing blow to the AJAs. Their country did not trust them and would not give them an opportunity to prove themselves as patriots. All the other services refused to draft or enlist them too!

Formation and Training
of the One Puka Puka Battalion

When the provisional Nisei troops were informed that they would be sent to the U.S. and organized as the 100th Infantry Combat Battalion, tears welled up in many a soldier's eyes, for now they would not be a labor detachment but an actual combat outfit, ready to show the enemy and other Americans that they were true citizens, willing to die for their country. True to their feelings, they chose "Remember Pearl Harbor" as their battalion slogan and nicknamed their unit as the "One Puka Puka" Infantry Battalion.[6] After they arrived in San Francisco, using three rail routes the members of the battalion were sent to their training base, Camp McCoy, Wisconsin.[7] There, they were assigned to various companies and once more completed the tedious routine of basic training.

An incident that illustrated the fighting fervor of the battalion occurred at McCoy when several Texans from the 2nd Infantry Division, then at McCoy, began calling the Niseis "Japs!" and "Yellow bellies!" These were fighting words and a royal battle ensued. Result: Thirty eight Texans hospitalized vs. one Nisei. The Nisei had many black belt judo masters and the Texans had been flung helter skelter.[8] In contrast, the local Wisconsinites, by and large, took kindly to the generally quiet and polite AJAs, and invited many to their homes for dinner. When the men wrote home describing the Wisconsin hospitality, the Japanese community in Hawaii sponsored, in deep appreciation,[9] a big luau open to all Wisconsin servicemen.

In mid-January 1943, the 100th Infantry Battalion was transferred to the deep south, Camp Shelby, Mississippi, for advanced unit training. Despite their small stature, five feet three inches being their average height, fully five inches below the average for American soldiers, the battalion's training accomplishments were remarkable.[10] After the Louisiana maneuvers, Major General Leslie J. McNair, Chief of Army Ground Forces, declared the 100th Battalion ready for overseas deployment, and by August 1943, they were on their way to North Africa. By September 1943 they were in the thick of fighting at Salerno, Italy.[11]

Formation of the
442nd Regimental Combat Team

From the moment of inactivation of the AJAs from the Territorial Guards a few days after Pearl Harbor, many young Nisei literally cried for an opportunity to shoulder weapons against the enemy. It was a deep and lasting insult to be classified 4C, "enemy alien," and not be drafted in the army or be accepted by the other services. With the spirit of *"gambare"* (never give up) taught them by their parents, those AJAs ousted from the Territorial Guards implored General Emmons to accept them in whatever capacity to help the war effort of Hawaii. Emmons, realizing the needs of Hawaii's military defenses, accepted them as a civilian volunteer work force. The youths promptly volunteered and called themselves the Varsity Victory Volunteers, since most were one time University of Hawaii ROTC cadets.[12]

As glowing training reports came in to the War Department and insistent correspondence arrived from the Japanese American Citizens League and the American Civil Liberties Union, both demanding that an AJA combat unit be formed, and with the backing of influential military leaders like General George C. Marshall, Admiral Chester Nimitz and Lieutenant General Delos Emmons, the War Department acquiesced. On 1 February, 1943, President Roosevelt announced from the White House that a volunteer combat infantry regiment would be formed from the AJA. This announcement was headlined in the local Hawaiian dailies and gleefully accepted by those in Hawaii, but was received with mixed emotions in the mainland AJA concentration camps.[13]

The initial call was for 2,500 volunteers. In Hawaii alone, over 11,000 men answered the call and this astounded the authorities. This phenomenal response to the call to arms can be traced to a number of reasons: the discrimination, suspicions, name callings, hatred shown—all these urged the Nisei to volunteer and to prove themselves as faithful, patriotic Americans. Consequently, the army formed a regimental combat team, the 442nd, that included an artillery battalion, engineer company, anti-tank company, cannon company, service company, medical detachment, and the regimental band, a total of over 4,000 men. By mid-April 1943, the men of the 442nd were in California, and then they were sent by trains, shades drawn, to Camp Shelby, Mississippi.[14] They chose as their regimental motto "Go For Broke" and this became their training and combat cry.[15]

Training of the
442nd Regimental Combat Team

As the Hawaii AJAs reached Camp Shelby, they were greeted by the white officers and mainland AJA NCOs (noncommissioned officers). Almost immediately friction arose between the Hawaiians and mainlanders since many of the NCO ranks had been assigned to the mainlanders. The mainlanders were derisively dubbed "Kotonks," and the Hawaiians were known by the mainlanders as the "Buddhaheads."[16] Occasional difficulties between these groups continued until a group of young Nisei women who were incarcerated with their families at Camp Jerome, Arkansas, came to a USO dance. Subsequent visits by select Hawaiian AJAs to the camp at Jerome "opened the eyes" of the Hawaiian Nisei soldiers, for now they came to understand the spartan and sad circumstances that mainland AJAs escaped from to serve America, an America that had taken them away from their homes, schools, jobs, and friends, an America that had deserted them.

With this eye-opener both sides allayed much of their misunderstandings and began the serious work of unit cohesion. In basic, advanced, unit and team training, the men of the 442nd displayed great enthusiasm and equaled the record of the 100th Infantry Battalion. In marches, marksmanship, hand-to-hand combat training, and maneuver-exercises, the 442nd was without equal. As they continued their training at Shelby, they performed brilliantly in morale and recreational activities, garnering championships in boxing, swimming, and baseball.

With training completed, the men of the 442nd left Camp

Shelby eagerly on 22 April, 1944. They were ready to prove that they were truly Americans. Simultaneously, their gallant brothers, the 100th Infantry Battalion, who had been tested in mortal combat around Cassino, were reassigned to aid in the heavy fighting then going on around Anzio.[17]

Combat and Heroism in
Italy, France, and Germany

Now, the 100th battalion was joined up with the 442nd. By the time the 100th arrived at Civiteveccia to join with the 442nd, it had suffered over 900 casualties and the wartime press had dubbed them the "Purple Heart" Battalion.[18] The 100th Battalion soldiers, who had seen steady combat since September, 1943, greeted their "younger brothers" with mixed emotions. They were happy to see the younger volunteers and they needed personnel. Already, they had over 400 Nisei replacements as casualties mounted. Despite their happiness to see them, however, older brothers who had experienced the horrors of war exclaimed in their pidgin patois, " Hey, you crazy! You stupid or what? You like mahke—this no game you know!"

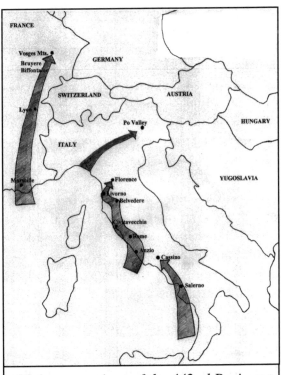

Major campaigns of the 442nd Regimental Combat Team

The men of the 100th knew well of what they spoke for they had fought courageously at Salerno, the Volturno River Crossing, through Benevento, to Cassino, Anzio and Rome.

The 442nd's Baptism of Fire: On 26 June, 1944, the 442nd was thrown into the battle for the town of Belvedere. Using double envelopment tactics, with the 100th in reserve initially, then having them attack aggressively from the rear, Belvedere was swiftly captured in nine hours, an objective that was to be captured in three days. Soon the town of Sasseta fell, and in July and August, Castellina, Colle Salvetti, Livorno and Pisa were captured by the hard charging Nisei warriors. General George C. Marshall remarked later: "I will say this about the Japanese fighting men in these units we had. They were superb! That word correctly describes it: Superb!"

The French Campaign: The fighting prowess of the Nisei became common knowledge among the field commanders, and General Jacob L. Devers, overall commander of American troops in France, had them transferred from Italy to France despite the strong objections of the 5th U.S. Army commander, General Mark Clark. The 100th/442nd landed in Marseilles on 30 September, 1944, and were transported by truck and train 450 miles north to the cold, damp, rugged, heavily forested Vosges Mountains. Now, they were but 100 miles from the Bavarian border. This was to be a completely new ball game, different from the rolling, rocky hills of sunny Italy; now it was, as remembered by one 442nd veteran, "mountains full of thick pine forests shrouded by chilling rain, fog, and sometimes fog and snow." Another vet remarked: "You couldn't see the enemy until you were about 50 yards away, while in Italy you could see them 300 yards away or more. The forest canopy blocked out so much light, it was dark during the day and pitch black at night."[19]

Rescue of the "lost" Texas Battalion: Into this setting the 442nd marched, nay, hiked and climbed, up the steep Vosges Mountains. After hard fighting they captured their objectives, the towns of Bruyeres and Biffontaine on 19 and 28 October, 1944, paving the way for the 7th U.S. Army to march into Germany. This was extremely dangerous fighting, much more so than the open grounds of Italy. "The enemy shells would hit the trees first and as they exploded hundreds of steel and wood fragments would come flying down—this is what caused so many casualties. Foxholes were useless against the tree bursts until they were covered with logs and dirt, but even those turned into death traps when the barrages buried them alive."[20]

Even before Biffontaine was formally taken, elements of the 100th, who were previously placed on a well deserved rest period, were on the move. Major General John Dahlquist of the 36th Infantry (Texas) Division had roused Colonel Charles Pence, the 442nd commander, to move the unit out to rescue one of his lost battalions, the 1st Battalion of the 141st Regiment. This was on the 27th of October. Dahlquist yelled, "that battalion is about to die and we've got to reach them!" The 2nd and 3rd Battalions of the 141st had tried and were unsuccessful in saving their buddies. The freezing weather, heavily wooded forests, road blocks, fox holes, mines, mortar and artillery barrages, interlocking machine gun and sniper fire, made the determined German defense almost impenetrable. The mountainous terrain made flanking moves impossible. Only the death defying frontal assault was possible. Without hesitation, Companies I and K of the 442nd, advancing along with the 100th, rose to a man, yelling and screaming. They made the famous "banzai" charge, firing from their hips, despite men falling all over the place." "Doc" Miyamoto, a medic, who was there, recalled with tears in his eyes, the wounded, gasping *"Kachan, Kachan, itai, itai"* — (Mama, Mama, it hurts, it hurts). Rudy Tokiwa, of K Company, commented, "In the battle for the lost battalion, every inch, every knoll and hill we took, we had to fight like hell. The Germans tried to stop us in every way they can. The lost battalion battle was the roughest battle I have ever been in. I never thought I'd live through it. I lost two of my best friends—Nakamura and Maeda."[21]

The ferocious battle was finally over on 30 October. As one eyewitness wrote: "Word was passed among the 1st Battalion men that fellow GI's had come to their rescue. The troops jumped out of their foxholes, smiled at the AJAs, and shook hands with our boys and said, 'You are our lifesavers. If it weren't for you God knows what would have happened to us."[22] Later, when General Dahlquist called for a formation to honor the 442nd, he asked Colonel Miller, "Where's all the men?" Miller said, "That's all that's left."

The "Lost Battalion" had 275 men when cut off by the Germans and the 442nd had rescued 211 of them. When the Vosges campaign began the 442nd Regiment had 2,943 men. After the rescue the 442nd was heavily depleted: 161 KIA, 2,000 WIA (882 were serious wounds), and 43 were missing. The regiment had dwindled to a third of its size. The 442nd RCT lost more in casualties than the number of Texans rescued but they got the job done. After the war, grateful Texans made the 442nd members "honorary Texans."[23] The 100th Battalion is an example of the tremendous losses that the 442nd suffered in this campaign. Ordinarily a company would have about 200 men. The following was the strength of the battalion after the rescue:

Company A= 67 men, 5 officers
Company B= 41 men, 5 officers
Company C= 66 men, 4 officers
Company D= 67 men, 7 officers [24]

General Dahlquist paid tribute to the men of the 442nd with these words:

During the past few weeks your fighting has been superb. It has been bitter and hard. You had to fight your way through some of the most difficult terrain in the world to your objective . . . . We have only the utmost admiration for you and what you have done . . . . No finer fighting, no finer soldierly qualities have ever been witnessed by the United States Army in its long history.[25]

This was unprecedented, deadly fighting for the brave unit. Of the seven presidential unit citations, four were given for the Vosges mountain battles.

On 28 March 1945, the 442nd was back in Italy at the special request of General Mark Clark, commander of the Fifth U.S. Army in Italy. The 442nd, now at full strength with added replacements, was assigned to spearhead the attack against Germany's vaunted Gothic Line. They were temporarily assigned to the 45th Infantry Division and later to the all black 92nd Infantry Division. The *Stars and Stripes* was effusive in its report as it headlined: THE 45TH'S ATTACK SPEARHEADED BY 442ND NISEI REGIMENT. The 45th Division headquarters "announced that the 442nd had performed 'brilliantly' in mopping up operations near Mt. Belvedere to the east of Massa."[26] On 5 April, 1944, the 442nd successfully attacked the mountainous, 3,000 foot high German lines by scaling the back side of the strong Gothic line. This they accomplished in the dead of night, surprising the defenders. After cracking the Gothic Line the 442nd continued attacking the German defenders along the Po River until war ended in Italy on 2 May, 1945. It was during this final campaign that then Lieutenant, now U.S. Senator Daniel Inouye, lost his right arm, as he led his platoon against an entrenched enemy position. It was during this campaign that Pfc. Sadao Munemori, heroically dove on top of a German hand grenade thrown into their dug-in position thereby saving two other Nisei comrades. For these acts of heroism, Inouye was decorated with the Distinguished Service Cross and Munemori was posthumously awarded the Congressional Medal of Honor.

Rescue of the Dachau Holocaust Victims: Prior to the regiment's return to Italy, the 522nd Artillery Battalion, the 442nd Regiment's artillery unit, was detached and sent to support the 7th U.S. Army's advance into southern Germany. Three of the first men to stumble into and discover the Dachau holocaust camps were forward observers, Tadashi Tojo, Robert Sugai and Shozo Kajioka.[27] According to unit historian, Hideo Nakamine, there were over thirty subcamps located around Dachau and the 522nd was the first to enter and rescue the victims. These subcamps were located at Augsburg, Bad Tolz, Munich, Salzburg, and Waachirken. Tojo commented in an interview: " We had no knowledge that camps like these ever existed during the war . . . the people were in striped prison garb lying on the snowy ground like dead men, their sexes indistinguishable because they were so emaciated." Kajioka reported that warehouses were filled with hills of shoes, adult's and children's. Some saw bodies stacked like cord-wood in railway cars. Ichiro Imamura, another 522nd veteran, commented that "prisoners were like skeletons and they shuffled weakly out of the compound and cut up dead cows on the road."[28] Today, the 522nd and its parent unit the 442nd RCT have set up a research committee which has documented the 522nd's role in the rescue of holocaust victims and they have been publicly honored by the Jewish holocaust victim's organization in Israel.[29]

The 100th/442nd Decorations and Awards

To this day the 442nd Regimental Combat Team is recognized as the most decorated unit for its size in the U.S. Armed Forces. Its record is incomparably superb, as seen in the listing of its honors and decorations.

Unit Decorations and Awards:

- 7 Presidential Distinguished Unit Citations (equivalent to a Distinguished Service Cross for the unit).
- 36 Army commendations.
- 87 Division Commendations.
- 18 decorations from Allied nations.

Individual Decorations:

- 9,486 Purple Hearts (for wounds or death in action).
- 1 Congressional Medal of Honor (for gallantry in action).
- 52 Distinguished Service Crosses (for exceptional heroism).
- 1 Distinguished Service Medal (exceptional meritorious service).
- 560 Silver Stars, with 28 Oak Leaf Clusters (gallantry in action).
- 22 Legion of Merit Medals (exceptionally meritorious

service).
- 15 Soldier's Medals (non-combat heroism).
- 4,000 Bronze Stars with 1,200 Oak Leaf Clusters (heroic or meritorious achievement.[30]

Epilogue

The Last Resting Places. The heroes of the 442nd are buried in distant parts of the world. Most remains were returned to Hawaii, and on the mainland, to private, state, or national cemeteries. A few were buried at the cemeteries closest to their battle sites, such as the American Cemetery at Epinal, and the Lorraine Cemetery near the Vosges mountain battle sites. A few of the parents and family members have made the long and sad journey to France to remember and honor their sons or brothers. The remains of six 442nd veterans were sent to Hiroshima, Yamaguchi, Niigata, or Okinawa prefectures in Japan to be buried beside their parents.

The Rich Legacy of the 442nd. When the guns of battle had cooled and they had returned to their homes, those on the mainland faced discrimination, racism, and even violence as many west coast citizens still harbored hatred against the AJAs. Nevertheless, the AJAs, pursuing higher education with a passion, progressed magnificently, both economically and socially. More and more they filtered into the wider suburban life, moving away from the "Little Tokyo" diasporatic ghettos. Several important events show how the Nisei soldier has helped AJAs become an integral part of American society.

First, the Walter-McCarran Act of 1952, gave the Issei immigrant parents an opportunity to finally apply for citizenship. During the active debates in Congress the pro-AJA arguments carried the day because of the tremendous respect all Americans had for the 442nd veterans and their supreme sacrifices. In Hawaii the winds of change occurred in 1954. Many 442nd veterans, abetted by continued higher education, supported the Democratic party and finally captured the

The Brothers in Valor monument dedicated to the men of the 100th Infantry Battallion, 442nd Regimental Combat Team, Military Intelligence Service and the 1399th Engineer Construction Battalion, in July, 1998, located at Fort Derussy, Hawaii

political leadership of Hawaii from the once entrenched Republican party. The AJAs had become staunch members of the Democratic party and came to occupy the governorship, the House and Senate leadership, as well as the county and municipal chairs. Politically, the AJAs had arrived because no one could even intimate that the Nisei were un-American and could not be trusted with governance. The record of the 442nd also played an important part in Hawaii finally achieving statehood in 1959, for it proved that the AJAs were truly Americans who paid with their bodies and blood for their share of America. Finally, the Civil Liberties Act of 1988 awarded AJAs incarcerated in the wartime concentration camps $20,000.

When the 442nd boys returned to Hawaii in 1945-6, they determined to keep alive the memory of their fallen comrades and the camaraderie developed during wartime by organizing the 100th Battalion and 442nd Clubs These clubs were organized on the four major islands, Oahu, Maui, Hawaii, and Kauai. They have been major activists and supporters in keeping alive the veteran's and political programs through effective educational and lobbying efforts. In March 1993, they sponsored the largest veterans' reunions seen in Hawaii when more than 6,000 442nd veterans arrived in Honolulu to celebrate the fiftieth anniversary.

Now, in the shadow of their golden years, the men of this illustrious combat unit have passed on their spirit and colors to their younger brethren. The U.S. Army, long since recognizing the brilliant history and record of the unit, has kept alive the colors, battle record and memory of the unit by retaining the 100th Battalion/442nd Infantry as a U.S. Army Reserve combat battalion. Though they are in their seventies, and even eighties, their heroic deeds will never be lost, as memorials in France, Germany, and Italy have been established. The sons and daughters of 442nd veterans have also organized themselves into clubs to educate future generations on the history and contributions of their parents to America. Books, booklets, films, video, interviews and articles have been written to remind all what President Harry S. Truman said in their honor as he presented them the seventh presidential unit citation: "You fought not only the enemy, you fought prejudice, and you have won. Keep up that fight, and continue to win, to make this great Republic stand for just what the Constitution says it stands for: the welfare of all the people, all the time."

Notes

1. Daniels, p.21.

2. California Congressman John H. Tolan, Mississippi Congressman John E. Rankin.

3. Tsukano, p.54.

4. Tsukano, p.57.

5. Duus, p.20.

6. In the Hawaiian language "puka" means a hole. A hole, being round as a zero, "100" became "one puka puka" in pidgin English.

7. Three routes, south, central, and north were utilized by the Army in order to allay any fears among the locals—white soldiers were assigned to guard them and the Niseis were told to pull down the shades so the local citizenry would not start a riot against them.

8. Duus, p.38.

9. Tsukano, p.85.

10. Heavy machine guns were set up in five seconds, while the U.S. military training manual indicated 16 seconds. Heavy machine gun squads, in full gear covered 3.3 miles in an hour during an eight-hour march despite their short legs compared to an average of 2.5 miles in an hour. Though obstacle courses had eight-foot fences, the small Nisei soldiers scaled the barriers easily.

11. *New York Times*, 3 October, 1943.

12. Duus, p.52. They were employed as civilian volunteer workers on road, barrack, defense construction for 11 months.

13. The writer remembers how, in his brother-in-law's family, all four of the eligible brothers answered the call to volunteer. By contrast, on the mainland many youths were sharply criticized by recalcitrant peers and elders for volunteering. They did not appreciate a country that would deprive them of all their rights.

14. Many parents had bade their sons a tearful good-bye but with the admonishment of "do your best for your country. If you die, so be it but never bring haji (shame) to your family name. Remember your Yamato damashi (Japanese spirit.)" Some even gave their sons the senninbari (the thousand stitch sash worn around the stomach to magically safeguard the soldier's well being).

15. "Go For Broke" is an oft-used Hawaiian pidgin slang phrase meaning "shoot the works, or give it your best!" Hawaiians used the phrase in shooting all their winnings in a crap game.

16. The term "kotonk" signified the sound that coconuts made as they fell to the ground from the tree. The Hawaii AJAs said Kotonks

were stubborn, empty headed, and "manini" (stingy, nonexpansive, non-group oriented). In turn the mainlanders called the tight, united Hawaii AJAs as "Buddha heads" referring to them as being more Japanese oriented in culture and language. Also, it could be more disparaging when they were called "Butaheads," with "buta" (pig) referring to the aggressive, brawling, ofttimes boorish Hawaii mannerisms.

17. Although assigned to the larger unit, the 442nd RCT, the 100th was not required to change its numerical designation.   General Charles Ryder, the 34th (Texas) Division commander, and General Mark Clark, 5th U.S. Army commander gave the unit special permission to retain the name it had honored with its notable battlefield victories.

18. Duus, p.158.

19. Oba, pp. 14-15.

20. Shimamura and Kawamoto, p.16.

21. Tsukano, p. 263.

22. Tsukano, p.269.

23. Duus, p. 216. At its peak strength the 442nd numbered 224 officers and 4,034 enlisted men (21 September, 1944).

24. Duus, p.216.

25. Tsukano, p. 272.

26, Duus, p.226.

27. *The Honolulu Advertiser*, pp. 21-22

28. Thelma Chang, pp. 197-198.

29. The author, in an August trip to the main Dachau death camp, viewed the plaque honoring the 522nd FA Bn/442nd RCT's role in rescuing the Dachau victims. Also in Hawaii Herald, "Chiune (Sempo) Sugihara: A Schindler of Japan," 7 October, 1994, pp. 1,10,

50

and 11.

30. "Go For Broke," The Honolulu Advertiser, 21 March, 1993, p.4.

Selected Bibliography

General

The Album, 442nd Combat Team, 1943.

Bosworth, Allan R., *America's Concentration Camps*, (New York, NY: W.W. Norton, 1967).

Chang, Thelma, *I Can Never Forget: Men of the 100th/442nd* (Honolulu, HA: Sigi Productions, Inc., 1991).

Conroy, Hilary and T. Scott Miyakawa, *East Across The Pacific* (Santa Barbara, CA: Clio Press, 1972).

Chuman, Frank F., *The Bamboo People: The Law And The Japanese Americans* (Del Mar, CA: Publishers Inc., 1976).

Daniels, Roger, *Concentration Camps U.S.A.* (New York, NY: Holt, Rinehart, and Winston, Inc., 1972).

Daniels, Roger and Harry Kitano, *Asian Americans* (Englewood Cliffs, NJ: Prentice Hall, 1988).

Duus, Masayo, *Unlikely Liberators: The Men Of The 100th And 442nd* (Honolulu, HA: University of Hawaii Press, 1987).

Grodzius, Morton, *Americans Betrayed* (Chicago, IL: University of Chicago Press, 1949).

Harrington, Joseph D., *Yankee Samurai*, (Detroit, MI: Pettigrew Enterprises, Inc., 1985).

Hosokawa, Bill, *Nisei: The Quiet Americans* (New York, NY,

William Morrow, 1969).

.

Japanese American Citizens League (JACL), The National Committee For Redress, *The Japanese American Incarceration: A Case For Redress*, (San Francisco, CA, 1978).

The Honolulu Advertiser, 21 March, 1993, "Holocaust Through Isle's Eyes," pp. 21-22.

Inouye, Daniel, with L. Elliott, *Journey To Washington*, (Englewood Cliffs, NJ: Prentice Hall, 1969).

Moulin, Pierre, *U.S. Samurais In Bruyeres* (Luxembourg: Rapid Press, 1993).

OBa, Ron, "Go For Broke," *The Honolulu Advertiser*, Special Section, 21 March, 1993.

National Japanese American Historical Society, "Americans of Japanese Ancestry and the United States Constitution" (San Franisco, CA: 1987).

New York Times, 3 October, 1943, "Japanese Americans: They Battle the Axis in Italy."

Pacific Citizen, Special Holiday Issue, December, 1984,"The Kibei."

Rocky Mountain MIS (Military Intelligence Service)Veterans Club, "Autobiographies," 1992.

Shimamura, Joe, and Shigeo Kawamoto, "Go For Broke: The Story of the 442nd Regimental Combat Team," *Pacific Press,* March, 1993

Stein, R. Conrad, "Nisei Regiment," in *World At War* (Chicago, IL: Children's Press, 1985).

Tsukano, John, *Bridge Of Love* (Honolulu, HA: Hawaii Hosts Inc., 1985).

Weglin, Michi, *Years Of Infamy: The Untold Story Of America's Concentration Camps* (New York, NY: William Morrow, 1976).

T.he Hawaii Herald, Vol. 14, No. 6, 19 March, 1993, "Saluting the Men of the 442nd RCT."

Audio-visual Media Sources

Ding, Loni, "The Color of Honor" (San Francisco, CA: Vox Productions, 1987).

_____, "Nisei Soldier," (San Francisco, CA: Vox Productions, 1987).

Kitano, Harry, "Relocations of Japanese Americans: Right or Wrong?" (Filmstrip, Zenger Productions, Inc.).

Narahara, Sheryl, "Fifty Years of Silence: The Untold Story of Japanese American Soldiers In The Pacific Theater, 1941-1952," (San Francisco, CA: National Japanese American Historical Society, 1993.

Military Intelligence Service (MIS) of Northern California and The National Japanese American Historical Society, "Mission In Manila," (San Francisco, CA: 1994).

Interviews

Anonymous, Company ___, ___ Battalion, 442nd RCT: "Yes, I volunteered and went from Shelby through all the campaigns in (Italy, to France (Vosges Campaign, 'Champaign Campaign',) and back to Italy (Gothic Line—Po Valley.) I was an infantryman, but not a hero—it was very, very rough!"

Oye, Tom, Company B, 100th Infantry Battalion, 442nd RCT: I was a replacement with the 100th. The Vosges Mountains campaign was my initiation into combat as an infantryman. It was awful with steel and tree splinters raining down on us—it was hell!"

Paul Shimizu, Company H, 2nd Battalion, 442nd RCT: "I was an original member of the 442nd. We greeted the Hawaii boys as they came into Camp Shelby. The training was very difficult but it sure prepared us for combat. After the Vosges campaign we were sent back to finish the combat in Italy. No, I don't know why our 522nd FA Battalion was sent to Germany—we sure missed them in Italy.

They had the 92d Division Artillery supporting our infantry but, hell, a lot of times they were very inaccurate, unlike our 522nd and they even dropped shells into our lines. I can truthfully say that the 442nd made our future life that much better because of the sacrifices and blood that we spilled for our country—America."

Yutaka Semba, 1st Battalion, 442nd, later 171st Infantry Battalion (Separate), and later with MIS (Military Intelligence Service): "I was with the 1st Battalion initially, but when the 100th began losing so many men, they began sending them replacements from our battalion. So, when the rest of the 442nd went overseas, they kept the 1st Battalion at Shelby to keep on training replacements. They then changed us to be the 171st Battalion (Separate). Then later on, about April of 1945, they were about to send us to Europe but the war soon ended. Some of us went overseas to Europe as Occupation Troops, but I volunteered to begin the study of Japanese so I ended up at Fort Snelling, Minnesota, at the Military Intelligence Service Language School in preparation for the Pacific War and Occupation duty in Japan. I never saw combat."

CHAPTER THREE

AMERICA'S SECRET WARRIORS

*Never in military history did an army know so much
about the enemy prior to actual engagement-"*
General Douglas MacArthur

*"Harry S. Truman said, 'They are our human secret weapons.' The
role that 6,000 Japanese American soldiers played in the Pacific
battlefield has been a well kept secret until now."*
Charles Hellinger
Los Angeles Times
20 July, 1982

"The 6000 Niseis shortened the Pacific war by two years."
Major General Charles Willoughby
G2 Intelligence Chief for
General MacArthur

*"As for the value of the Nisei I couldn't have gotten along without
them."*
Major General Frank D. Merrill,
Commander of Merrill's
Marauders in Burma

*"By these brave people, the lives of several thousand Americans
were saved."*
Colonel Sydney F. Mashbir
Commander of ATIS
(Allied Translator and Interpreter Section)

Introduction

Americans, especially World War II buffs, are aware of the
wartime contributions and fighting ability of the Japanese
Americans, the "Nisei soldiers," who fought heroically in
Europe as members of the l00th Infantry Battalion and the 442nd

Regimental Combat Team. This essay, therefore, is about another segment of Japanese American soldiers, the almost forgotten Military Intelligence Service (MIS) men.

First, some background. In Hawaii, prior to 7 December, 1941, the day of the Japanese bombing of Pearl Harbor, there were approximately 163,000 persons who were ethnic Japanese. On the mainland the number was 120,000. Two thirds were *Nisei*, the offspring of the immigrant parents, who were known as the *Issei*. The *Kibei*, another term to be used in this essay, represented the small number of Nisei who were educated and brought up in Japan during their formative years.[1] Even prior to the actual beginning of the war, all ethnic Japanese were suspect by the U.S. military authorities and, in fact, shortly after the tragic attack, Japanese Americans in the Hawaii Territorial Guards[2] were unceremoniously cashiered out of their Guard service. On the mainland, the infamous incarceration of Japanese Americans began when Executive Order 9066 was issued on 19 February, 1942. Americans of Japanese Ancestry (AJA) were no longer to be drafted and all the services would not enlist any AJA. Those who had already been drafted were not allowed to be in combat units and many were transferred out from line status and placed in supernumerary or general labor category.[3] As a result of all of this, the spirit and general morale of the AJAs, as can be well understood, were at rock bottom.

As America prepared for war, however, senior military intelligence officers reached the appalling conclusion that we were bereft of any Japanese linguists, those who could speak, read and write Japanese. American Caucasian personnel who were adept in Japanese could be counted on the fingers of one hand. Those who were even vaguely familiar with the language were few, too, and they were primarily children of missionaries who lived in Japan before the war. Nevertheless, credit goes to the senior army intelligence officers[4] who foresaw the impossible situation of engaging an enemy without personnel able to decipher Japanese, a difficult language at best. These officers saw a possible solution to this problem in the Nisei. After all, weren't they speaking to their immigrant parents in Japanese and weren't they also going to Japanese language schools after finishing their daily English public school classes?

The draftee army of 1940-41 did include a proportion of AJAs. They were surveyed and the results were appalling—only fifty eight were deemed suitable. In November, 1941, 60 soldiers—58 Niseis and two Caucasians, became the first class of the Military Intelligence Service Language School (MISLS).[5] The small number available for schooling clearly reflected that the acculturation of the Nisei to American culture had progressed far beyond what most persons might have believed.

The school began in an old, abandoned airplane hangar at Crissey Field, Presidio of San Francisco, on a budget of two thousand dollars. Everything—desks, chairs, chalkboards, chalk, paper, etc.—were scrounged from the main post. Instructors made their own teaching manuals and taught only from past experiences. This was a very difficult situation since *heigo* (Military Japanese), advanced *kanji* (Chinese characters), reading and writing, and *sosho* (continuous cursive Japanese writing, sometimes called grass writing), were constants in Japanese orders, documents, diaries, letters, and coded messages.[6] The Kibei were especially needed in mastering this difficult form of advanced Japanese. The attack on Pearl Harbor and the issue of Executive Order 9066 on 19 February, 1942, which called for the expulsion of all ethnic Japanese from the west coast, required the army to look elsewhere to conduct the MI school. Under these circumstances, the state of Minnesota was chosen as the next location for the Military Intelligence Service Language School since the state was known for its kindly outlook towards all ethnic and racial categories.

Camp Savage and Fort Snelling

Camp Savage, in the town of Savage, Minnesota, was a one time CCC (Civilian Conservation Corps) and, later, a state maintained old-men's camp. This became the sparse new home of the MISLS, and many of the Hawaii and California MIS veterans remember with pain the severity of their first winter in Minnesota.

The first class at Savage began with 200 students. Meanwhile thirty five of the original sixty members of the San Francisco class were scattered into combat units from the Aleutians to Australia. As the Pacific bat-

Military Intelligence Service Language School, Ft. Snelling, MN, 1945. Building in front is Company F, followed by Company C.

tles continued from 1942 into 1943 (Guadalcanal, Attu and Tarawa), and as these "guinea pig" linguist specialists began to show their worth, division, corps, and joint forces commanders began requesting, and even commandeering, the Nisei linguists.[7] By January 1944, over a thousand (1,101) students were enrolled at Savage and soon it became evident that expansion of the school was absolutely necessary to meet combat needs. Fortunately, an old time regular army post was located close by with adequate facilities and so the move was made in August, 1944, to Fort Snelling, Minnesota. Fort Snelling's commodious buildings and enviable Twin Cities location was the site of the MISLS until it was moved to the Presidio of Monterey in July of 1946. By this time over 6,000 students had graduated from this service school.

In the initial stages of the school many graduates received only hurried basic training and were immediately shipped overseas. Time and their language expertise overruled special combat or team/unit training. Later, as the war dragged on, special requirements necessitated that some obtain paratrooper training, or special radio intercept classes and technical intelligence training. The MIS school routine and class studies were extremely demanding.

Permanent officer's quarters, Fort Snelling Minnesota, Winter, 1945

Mondays through Fridays were devoted to classroom work and this included required night classes until 9 p.m. The "school of the soldier," to include the ubiquitous inspections, were held on Saturdays. Sundays continued to be the traditional sabbath day. Since heigo (military Japanese) proved to be difficult even for the knowledgeable Kibei, many students continued their study in the latrine after lights were extinguished. Some even continued their study with a flashlight under their blankets. Such dedication was commonplace.

Niseis to the Rescue

In the earlier phases of the war little was known of the contributions of the Nisei linguists by the other services, and the United States Navy and Marines had even barred them from enlisting or being attached to their units. They did not trust the Nisei. But as the Pacific battles continued and their value as intelligence personnel became evident (as interrogators, interpreters, translators, psychological operations broadcasters, cave flushers, decoders, etc.), and as the U.S. Army experienced the tremendous value of having Nisei as their eyes and ears, the other services began to clamor for Nisei linguists.

In fact, even the British, Australian and New Zealand armies demanded Nisei language personnel.[8]

Richard Sakakida

The story of the Niseis in combat in the Pacific is replete with many instances of bravery, gallantry, and heroism, of the remarkable, unflinching loyalty of a minority to their mother country. One such hero was Richard Sakakida. Young Richard Sakakida was recruited by the U.S. Army Counter Intelligence Police prior to Pearl Harbor and sent to Manila, Philippines.[9] Mission: to spy on the Japanese businessmen located in Manila. Ironically, our army intelligence in Hawaii focused on the Philippines as the probable attack point during those threatening days prior to the Pearl Harbor attack, and they felt that the businessmen would have first hand knowledge of their military's intentions.

When the war did begin, Sakakida rejoined his unit and served courageously in the defense of Bataan and Corregidor. As General Douglas MacArthur and some of his higher headquarters staff personnel left the Philippines by air, he, as a valued linguist, was offered the final seat on the last plane to go to Australia. He declined, offering up his seat to a married AJA linguist, and continued serving our cause as the personal interpreter to Lieutenant General Jonathan Wainwright. After the surrender of the Philippines, Sakakida was imprisoned and interrogated daily in brutal fashion. The Japanese accused him of spying against Japan. "How could you be a traitor to your race and heritage and work against your mother country and for the Americans!" Sakakida held true to his faith in and loyalty to America and steadfastly denied being a spy—all this despite daily torture that included being stripped naked with his hands tied behind his back and stretched upwardly by rope around a rafter so that he barely touched his toes on the floor. Then, nefariously, they applied lighted matches or cigarettes to his inner thighs and gradually worked up to his buttocks and private parts.

Through all this Sakakida persevered always claiming to be

an American soldier and not a spy.[10] This story does not end here. The Japanese had eventually transferred him to one of the Filipino POW camps. With his knowledge of the Japanese military discipline, habits, and culture he cleverly ingratiated himself to the camp commandant and the guards. He stole Japanese uniforms, equipment, and rifles, and had some Filipino POWs pose as the Japanese prison guards. He marched his Filipino guards to the main gate, overcame the Japanese guards and subsequently 500 Filipinos escaped into the jungles.[11] Sakakida melted into the jungles and continued to feed Filipino guerrillas information about Japanese units to the end of the war. Sakakida spent more than a year in the jungles of Luzon and was finally rescued despite being wounded, emaciated and disease ridden. Unfortunately, Sakakida was awarded only the bronze star for his wartime heroism and exploits against the enemy.[12]

Nisei Linguists in Combat

The Niseis took every advantage of the Japanese arrogant notion that their language was too complicated for an ordinary Occidental to exploit. The Japanese often sent messages in the clear, or in a simple *kana* code. The shooting down of the redoubtable Admiral Isoroku Yamamoto is a case in point. Nisei linguist Harold Fudenna, in Port Moresby, New Guinea, intercepted the radio call concerning Yamamoto's inspection trip of his forces in Bouganville and immediately notified higher headquarters. Other Nisei linguists stationed in Alaska and Hawaii had also heard the call and so it was arranged for a P-38 fighter plane ambush of Yamamoto's twin engine "Betty" bomber and the six zero escort planes. The P-38s, coming from Henderson Field in Guadalcanal, had but fifteen minutes flying time over northern Bouganville but the planning was so precise that Yamamoto's plane was shot down.[13]

Another event that truly showed the inestimable worth of the Nisei was their superb translation of Japan's "Z" plan. Operation "Z" was Japan's intended, all-out counterattack plan against the U.S. Navy in the Central Pacific. This was to be her major, last-gasp effort and she had mobilized her remaining capital ships and air effort for this battle. On 31 March, 1944, the two Japanese bombers transporting Admiral Mineichi Koga (Yamamoto's successor) and his chief of staff, Vice Admiral Shigeru Fukudome crashed into the sea off the southern coast of the Philippines during a severe tropical storm. Admiral Koga perished and Admiral Fukudome's waterproof container, which completely outlined Japan's Operation "Z," was picked up by Filipino fishermen and turned in to U.S. headquarters by the guerrillas. The front-line Niseis, realizing the strategic import of the document, had it immediately transported by submarine and aircraft to Allied Translator Interpreter Section headquarters at Brisbane, Australia. There, at ATIS, two of the best Kibei translators, Yoshikazu Yamada and George Sankey, along with three Caucasian officers that included Faubion Bowers (later to become MacArthur's personal interpreter), translated the entire document.[14]

ATIS sent a copy to Admiral Nimitz at Pearl Harbor and he had copies sent to every flag officer in the Pacific. Japan was completely unaware that their Operation "Z" plan had been compromised, and as the American forces began their invasions of Saipan, Tinian and Guam in June, 1944, Admiral Spruance's carrier fleet and submarines dealt the Imperial Japanese fleet a devastating defeat. We knew their every move. And so, during the Battle of the Philippines Sea, our forces shot down a record 346 planes on 19 June, 1944, the so-called "Marianas Turkey Shoot."[15]

Sergeants Matsumoto and Kubo

The Nisei proved their combat worthiness in many other ways. Sergeant Kenji Yasui came to be known as the "Little Sergeant York" when he volunteered to swim to an enemy held island on the Irrawaddy River in Burma. With his platoon out of sight he strode to the center of the island and commanded in Japanese, "I am Colonel Yamamoto of the Imperial Japanese Army. I have come to take you on a secret mission. Follow me." No one followed, so he repeated his order and soon seventeen Japanese soldiers came forth. He put

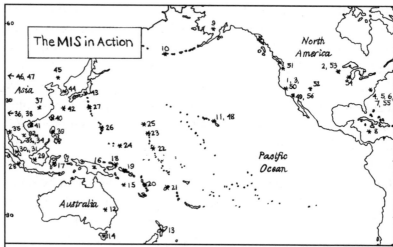

Sites of the Military Intelligence Service activities of key significance to the U.S. war effort (Source: Unsung Heroes, MIS NW Association).

The MIS In Action—Map Legend

1. MISLS at Presidio of San Francisco, California
2. MISLS at Camp Savage and Fort Snelling, MN
3. ALS-DLI at Presidio of Monterey, CA
4. Washington, D.C.
   Pentagon
   Fed. Comm Comm.
5. Camp Ritchie, MD
6. New York
7. Virginia
   Fort Holabird
   Vint Hill Farms Stn.
8. Caribbean Sea
9. Alaska
10. Aleutians
    Kodiak
    Adak
    Dutch Harbor
    Kiska
    Attu
11. Hawaii
12. Australia
13. New Zealand
14. Tasmania
15. Coral Sea Islands

16. New Guinea
    Biak
    Japen
    Ambon
    Buru
17. Celebes-Halmahera-Molotai
18. Bismarck Archipelago
    Rabaul
    Bougainville
    Green Islands
    Admiralty Is.
    Buka
    New Ireland
    New Britain
19. Solomon Is.
    Guadalcanal
    Malaita
    Santa Isabel
    Vella Lavella
    New Georgia
20. New Hebrides-New Caledonia-Espiritu Santo
21. Fiji Islands-Samoa-Tahiti
22. Gilbert Islands
    Tarawa
    Makin

23. Marshall Islands
    Kwajalein
    Eniwetok
    Ponape
    Bikini
24. Caroline Islands
    Truk
    Palau
    Yap
25. Wake Island
26. Mariana Islands
    Guam
    Rota
    Saipan
    Tinian
27. Iwo Jima
28. Sumatra-Java
29. Borneo-Sarawak
30. Singapore
31. Malay
32. Vietnam
33. Cambodia
34. Thailand
35. Burma
36. India
37. China
38. Nepal
39. The Philippines

40. Taiwan
41. Hong Kong
42. Okinawa-Ryukyu Is.
43. Japan
44. Korea
45. Manchuria
46. France
47. Germany
48. MIS Veteran's Club, Hawaii
49. MIS Club of So. CA, L.A., CA
50. MIS Assoc. of N. CA, San Fran., CA.
51. MIS-Northwest Assoc., Seattle, WA
52. Rocky Mountain MIS Veterans of MN, Mpls., MN
53. Japanese American Veterans of MN, Mpls., MN
54. The American Legion Chicago Nisei Post #1183, Chicago, IL
55. Japanese American Veteran's Assoc. of Washington, D.C.
56. Nisei Women's Army Corps, Los Angeles, CA

them through close order drill and when some threatened four POWs they were killed and he ordered the other thirteen to swim and push him across the river as he stood atop the raft.[16]   Sgt. Yasui was awarded the silver star for his 1944 "show of bravery."

Sergeant Roy Matsumoto's heroic exploits with Merrill's Marauders in Burma is another case in point. On 4 March, 1944, Matsumoto crawled within hearing distance of a Japanese unit about to attack. He hurried back to his defending unit to inform his commander of the impending attack. An ambush was set up and as the Japanese moved to their attack position Matsumoto shouted in Japanese "*Susume! Susume!*" ("Charge! Charge!"). The premature attack resulted in 54 enemy dead and no American casualties. Matsumoto was awarded the Legion of Merit medal.

One month later Matsumoto and the Marauders were completely surrounded at Nphum Ga, Burma. In the midst of the Japanese assault he stood up and, posing as a Japanese officer, ordered a fatal "Banzai" suicide charge into the strong point of the U.S. defense line. The fact that Matsumoto survived is a miracle and the Marauder survivors all felt that he had saved their lives. When quizzed why Matsumoto was not put in for the Congressional Medal of Honor the commanding officer remarked, "He was only an enlisted man doing his duty."[17]

Sergeant Bob Hoichi Kubo received the Distinguished Service Cross for his bravery on a cave-flushing mission in Saipan. There were approximately 24,000 civilians in Saipan, eighty six percent of whom were Japanese. Learning from a POW that Japanese soldiers were holding a large number of civilians captive in a cave, Kubo slid down a rope into the cave and laid down his .45 caliber pistol before the Japanese soldiers. Then he shared his K-rations with the hungry soldiers and coolly talked them into surrendering. Kubo then led the soldiers and more than 100 civilians out of the cave. This occurred at the time when hundreds of civilians, especially mothers with their young in hand, were committing suicide by jumping into the raging sea hundreds of feet below because they had been indoctrinated by the Japanese propaganda that Americans were rapacious, abominable monsters.[18]

Interrogation Techniques of the Nisei

Initially, U.S. interrogation of Japanese POWs emphasized the strict, overbearing, dictatorial "you-do-as-I-command-or-else!" approach. This was the method used against the Germans. Nisei linguists, however, perceptive of Japanese traits, demonstrated kindness and understanding, making timely and appropriate use of food and tobacco to gain valuable information. After all, the Japanese soldier was trained to fight and die for the emperor. Their service schooling did not include prisoner of war conduct; one was to fight to the very last. So Nisei interrogators always made sure that the POW was fed, clothed, cleaned up, and reassured that he would not be abused and destroyed. Once reassured, the prisoner literally "spilled his guts out" in keen appreciation. Enemy positions, weapons emplacements, ammo caches, names of commanders, officers and NCOs, unit tactics, the order of battle—all were readily obtained by the interrogators. Our forces were thereby able to accomplish ambushes successfully and the field commanders continuously praised and repeated the dictum that the Nisei were the eyes and ears of our front line units.[19]

MIS Linguists in Occupation of Japan

With the end of the shooting war on 15 August, 1945, the language focus shifted to the Occupation of Japan. *Heigo* (military terminology) was out and civil Japanese, along with military and government terminology and policies, were stressed, both in training and in the field. Here, again, America's occupation of Japan could not have succeeded so smoothly without the language expertise and presence of the Nisei. They were the bridge of understanding between the democracy espousing America and the militaristic Japan. During the occupation, Japanese citizens marveled at the role played by the Nisei, for they came to be MacArthur's spearhead in our thrust to democratize Japan.[20]

The Military Intelligence Service Language School (MISLS)

at Fort Snelling, Minnesota, continued a fresh supply of linguists overseas as replacements for the many other combat linguists who returned home deservedly. Following MacArthur's 3-D edicts (destruction, demobilization, and democracy), Nisei soldiers accompanied their American officers and civilian leaders all throughout Japan to explain and aid the Japanese in understanding our occupa-

Nisei Soldiers, Sgts. Asahino and Yoshika enjoying friendship of Mrs. Iwabuchi, a Japanese national.

tion program.

Niseis served honorably in undertaking the destruction phase of the once potent Japanese war machine; not only did they uncover hidden ammo caches and dumps, but they tracked down elements of Zaibatsu war production factories which were not fully destroyed. Also, Nisei interpreters and translators helped investigate and apprehend war criminals, both class A and B types. Some participated in the prosecution or defense of these criminals. An interesting episode related by Sergeant James Tanabe recalled how he was at the botched suicide attempt of Premier General Hideki Tojo and saved the general's life by donating his blood as Tojo's life waned in the balance. He subsequently became Tojo's personal prison guard until Tojo was hanged by order of the International War Crimes Tribunal.[21]

In the demobilization phase the Nisei were employed to hasten and smooth the process by which over eight million overseas Japanese soldiers and civilians were brought back to their homeland. Of crucial importance was their service as counterintelligence agents who spotted and ferreted out communist agents who had been recruited while prisoners after the war in Siberia. The major port of entry for these repatriates was Maizuru in southwestern Japan.

The True Value of the Nisei Soldiers

A major purpose of this essay is to impress upon the reader the truly heroic exploits of the AJA soldier in the Pacific war. Their value to the United States during World War II is inestimable. General C. H. Willoughby, MacArthur's intelligence chief, said: "The Nisei saved a million lives and shortened the war by two years." Long time United States Senator Daniel Inouye, who fought valiantly in Europe with the other major AJA unit, the 442nd RCT, said in the 50th Anniversary reunion of the MIS vets:

> We (Nisei) all started together when Pearl Harbor exploded, pushed by EO 9066 into camps, not fit to be drafted until the president opened the draft. The turnout was unprecedented, but here is where those of you here took another lonely step forward, serving without public recognition, serving with men who were suspicious of you, or who hated you....We had an easy field; we knew what our enemy looked like but you didn't, and to that the stories of the 442nd fighting in Europe made the news, but there was very few for the Nisei in the Pacific engaged in military intelligence. We need to correct and acknowledge you, the Nisei in MIS are the real heroes. I have great admiration for you and your contributions. As a matter of honor, why would anyone take the assignment that you took? [22]

Thousands of Nisei, despite incarceration of themselves and their families in hastily set up camps in deserts, swamps and high mountain plateaus, god forsaken, and treated as prisoners, still volunteered or were drafted to serve in combat against their ancestral roots. They were willing to die for America, their birth-land and many died fighting for values that they believed in — individual freedom, dignity, loyalty, honor, and duty to country. They wanted to prove that American culture is not a matter of skin color but one of character, faith and loyalty to their nation.

Epilogue

Fifty years after their war experiences, many of America's samurai warriors are in their golden years and thousands more have since departed. What have their pains and sacrifices brought forth? How have they made it better for the AJAs of today? Are the present AJAs and other Asian Americans appreciative of the great sufferings experienced by these WWII veterans? The Freedom of Information Act of 1974 allowed many of the secret documents that the Nisei linguists translated to be viewed by the public.[23] Yet, the Niseis through past customs of reticence (known as *enryo* in Japanese) failed to let the public know of their worthy exploits. Now, gradually, they have come to realize the historical significance of bestowing their legacy to the future AJAs. The reunion panel-discussions and subsequent write-ups, be they autobiographical sketches, unit histories, news and magazine articles, books and videos, have been sincere, edifying, and, often, gripping episodic look-sees into the Nisei Yankee samurai. They were brave soldiers who served and fought hard to win the right to be called Americans.

Notes

1. Approximately two thirds were American citizens, their parents were known as *Issei* (first generation), and they were born in Japan. Their children, American citizens by birth, are called *Nisei* (second generation), the grandchildren are called *Sansei* (third) and the great grandchildren are called *Yonsei* (fourth generation.)

2. The Hawaii Territorial Guard (HTG) had been organized to do home security duty when the Hawaii National Guard was federalized in 1941, prior to Pearl Harbor.

3. Harrington, p.33.

4. Brigadier General John Weckerling (then Lieutenant Colonel), and Colonel Kai E. Rasmussen (then Captain).

5. Testing was then expanded to include those in Hawaii and those incarcerated in the relocation camps. Of the 3,700 surveyed only 3% were accomplished in Japanese, another 4% were proficient, and a further 3% could be useful only after a prolonged period of schooling.

6. Weckerling, p.187.

7. Nisei linguists proved their immense worth in translating the enemy's Midway and Marianas Battle plans, as well as accompanying the U.S. Marines and Army invasion units into Guadalcanal, Attu, Kiska, Tarawa, Gilbert and Marshall Islands, New Guinea, Iwo Jima, Okinawa, etc. (*The Pacific War And Peace,* pp. 17, 27-29, 38, 43, 51).

8. *The Pacific War And Peace,* pp. 58-59.

9. Harrington, p. 4.

10. Lieutenant Colonel Richard Sakakida (USAF Retired), gave this poignant, courageous report orally at the MIS National Reunion, Monterey, California, 31 October 1992.

11. Harrington, p.115.

12. *The Pacific War And Peace*, p. 14. On 17 February, 1999, Sakakida was posthumously awarded the Distinguished Service medal for his heroic WWII work in the Philippines.

13. *The Pacific War And Peace,,* p. 38.

14. Yoshikazu, Yamada, "My War Time Experiences," MIS Veterans Club of Hawaii, 50th Anniversary Reunion 8-10 July 1993.

15. Yoshikazu, Yamada, "My War Time Experiences," Sunao Ishio, quoted in "The MIS Story," *Rafu Shimpo,* 12 November 1993, P.5.

16. Ishimaru Military Intelligence Service Language School, U.S. Army, TecCom Production, Los Angeles, CA., 1991., p.18.

17. *The Pacific War And Peace*, p.62.

18. Ishimaru, Military Intelligence Service Language School, U.S. Army, p. 18.

19. John Aiso, p. 80.

20. The author served with the Occupation Forces in 1947-48. Japanese often remarked that America was truly a great country in

even allowing ethnic Japanese Nisei to serve as officers, noncommissioned officers and soldiers in the victorious U.S. armed forces.

21. Sergeant James Tanabe's account of Premier General Tojo's imprisonment at Sugamo Prison, Tokyo, given at the MIS Capital Reunion, Washington D.C., 21-23 October 1993.

22. U.S. Senator Daniel Inouye, guest speaker, MIS Capital Reunion, Washington D.C., 21-23 October 1993.

23. Over 3 million documents were translated.

Selected Bibliography

Books

Chuman, Frank F., *The Bamboo People: The Law And Japanese-Americans* (Del Mar, CA: Publishers Incorporated, 1976).

Daniels, Roger, *Concentration Camps U.S.A.: Japanese Americans And World War II* (New York, NY: Holt, Rinehart and Winston, Inc., 1972).

Duus, Masayo U., *Unlikely Liberators, The Men Of The 100th And 442nd* (Honolulu, HA: University of Hawaii Press, 1987).

Harrington, John D., *Yankee Samurai: The Secret Role Of Nisei In America's Pacific Victory* (Detroit, MI: Pettigrew Enterprises, 1979).**

Hosokawa, Bill, *Nisei: The Quiet Americans* (New York, NY: W. Morrow Inc., 1969).*

Ichinokuchi, Tad, ed., with Daniel Aiso, *John Aiso And The MIS: Japanese American Soldiers In The Military Intelligence Service, World War II* (Los Angeles, CA: MIS Club of So. CA., 1988).**

Ishimaru, Stone S., *Military Intelligence Service Language School: U.S. Army* (Los Angeles, CA: TecCom Productions, 1991).*

Ishimaru, Stone S., *Military Intelligence Service Language School: Camp Savage, Minnesota 1942-1944* (Los Angeles, CA: MIS Club of So. California, 1992).*

Moulin, Pierre, *U.S. Samurai In Bruyeres*, (Luxembourg, France, Rapid Press, 1993).

Ota, Masahide, *The Battle Of Okinawa: The Typhoon Of Steel And Bombs* (Tokyo, Japan: Kume Publishing Co., 1984).

The Pacific War And Peace: Americans Of Japanese Ancestry In The Military Intelligence Service, 1941-1952, MIS Association of Northern California and The National Japanese American Historical Society, 1991.**

Tsukano, John, *Bridge Of Love* (Honolulu, HA: Hawaii Hosts, Inc., 1985).

Turner, David, *Legacy Of Merrill's Marauders* (Turner Publishing Co., 1987).

Yoshida, Jim, with Bill Hosokawa, *The Two Worlds Of Jim Yoshida* (New York, NY: William Morrow & Co., Inc., 1972).

Albums, Newspapers, Other Publications

Americans Of Japanese Ancestry And The United States Constitution (San Francisco, CA: National Japanese-American Historical Society, 1987).

Autobiographies (Rocky Mountain MIS Veterans Club, 1992).

"50 Years of Excellence," (Presidio of Monterey, Defense Language Institute, Public Affairs Office, 50th Anniversary 1941-1991, 1 November, 1991).

"The Kibei," in *Pacific Citizen*, Special Holiday Issue, Vol. 99, No. 25, 21-18 December, 1984 (Monterey Park, CA).

"The Men of the Military Intelligence Service." (Honolulu, HA:*The Hawaii Herald*, Vol. 5, No. 18, 21 September, 1984).

"The Military Intelligence Service," (Honolulu, HA: *The Hawaii Herald,* Vol.. 14, No. 13, 2 July 1993).

MIS Capital Reunion, "The Nisei Veteran: An American Patriot," Washington D.C., 21-23 October 1993. (Interviews and Program).

THE MISLS ALBUM, U.S. War Department General Staff, Washington D.C., 1946).

MIS Club of So. California Newsletter, Vol. 8, No. 6, November/December, 1993 (Los Angeles, CA: MIS Club of So. California).

MIS Club of So. California Newsletter, Vol. 9, No. 1, January/February, 1994 (Los Angeles, CA: MIS Club of So. California).

MIS 50th Anniversary Hawaii Reunion, Honolulu, 7-10 July 1993.

(Interviews and Program).

"MIS, Part I," in *Pacific Citizen*, Vol. II 7, No. 16, 5-11 November, 1993(Monterey Park, CA).

"MIS, Part II," in *Pacific Citizen*, Vol. II 8, No. 17, 12-18 November, 1993 (Monterey Park, CA)

MIS 50th Anniversary Sentimental Journey Reunion, Minneapolis, MN., 28-30 May 1992. (Interviews and Program).

San Francisco and Monterey, CA: The MIS 50th Anniversary Reunion Program, 29 October-2 November, 1991.

Savage Review, Vol. 8, No. 9, May, 1992 (Savage, MN).

"Secret Soldiers," (Honolulu, HA: *The Honolulu Advertiser*, 4 July 1993, p.1).

Yamashita, Nob, "Fighting My Ancestors: An Autobiography" in *MIS Club of So. California Newsletter*, Vol. 8, No. 7, Christmas Edition, 1993, p. 7-8 (Los Angeles, CA: MIS Club of So. California).

Audio-visual Media Sources

Ding, Loni, "The Color of Honor," (San Francisco, CA: Vox Productions, 1987).

Kitano, Harry, "Relocation of Japanese Americans: Right or Wrong?," (Culver City, CA., Zenger Productions, Inc.).

Narahara, Sheryl K., "Fifty Years of Silence: The Untold Story of Japanese American Soldiers in the Pacific Theater, 1941-1952," (San Francisco, CA: National Japanese American Historical Society, 1993).

CHAPTER FOUR

KAMIKAZE: JAPAN'S MOST BIZARRE WORLD WAR II WEAPON

O ver half a century ago Japan, faced with inevitable defeat to the overwhelming human and material resources of the Allied forces, unleashed the most unorthodox battle tactic ever faced by any naval forces, the Kamikaze suicidal plane. By August, 1944, Japan had suffered losses in the Aleutians, the Caroline and Marshall Islands, the Marianas (Saipan, Tinian, and Guam), and the Battle of the Philippines Sea,[1] and the U.S. was poised to invade the Philippines through Leyte Island. The aim of this essay is to investigate and explain the circumstances and reasons why Japan initiated this new, seemingly insane operation. Why did they go into suicidal attacks? How did they do it? What was their training and psychological make-up? What were the results? This essay will resolve all these questions.

Japan's War Expansionism
May 1942-October 1944

By May, 1942, Imperial Japan stretched from China, Manchuria, Korea, Southern Sakhalin, Aleutians (Attu, Kiska), Wake Island, Caroline/Marshall Islands, Dutch East Indies, French Indochina, to Burma. This huge empire, primarily established by the army during the first six months after Pearl Harbor, was being steadily whittled away by the U.S. forces after our navy's spectacular victory in the Midway battle, 2-4 June, 1942.

After the Philippines Sea battle where young Japanese pilots were shot down like ducks in a shooting gallery, the Imperial Japanese Navy admirals were terror stricken. With the capture of Saipan and Tinian, Americans were within striking distance of Tokyo and the rest of the home islands.[2] American offensive moves were easily foreseeable: Philippines, then Formosa, the Ryukyus after that, and soon thereafter the home islands of Japan. Admiral Soemu Toyoda, successor to the fallen Admiral Yamamoto, had husbanded his ships and forces. He had over one hundred combat vessels and could bank on over one thousand fighter planes. But if the Japanese continued with their old defensive tactics their resources would be destroyed in no time. Realizing their desperate status, several navy leaders began advocating desperate measures.[3] They argued that it was a now or never situation. By 7 July, 1944, army officers, too, were considering the use of suicide attacks by air along with Admiral Ohnishi,[4] the acknowledged engineer of the tactic. Ohnishi argued:

> We must initiate a new attack method. Look, our pilots are young and inexperienced—even before they reach the target site they are shot down by the overwhelming U.S. fighter planes.[5] Since they are going to die any way, why not have them purposefully ram enemy ships and destroy American ships and lives. One Japanese pilot and plane for an American ship and American lives. Let's impress upon all pilots the desperate situation facing imperial Japan and call for volunteers to step forth and save our fatherland.

After the Battle of the Marianas (Saipan, Tinian, Guam) of July and August, 1944, Captain Eiichiro Jyo, commander of the carrier *Chiyoda*, remarked: "No longer can we hope to sink the numerically superior enemy aircraft carriers through ordinary attack methods. I urge the immediate organization of special attack units to carry out crash-dive tactics, and I ask to be placed in command of them."[6]

Thus was the suicide corps born. These were desperate times for Japan. By 1944 the Japanese home front was being bombed daily, bringing destruction, fires, and death all over. Now the Buddhist and Shinto priests were called upon incessantly by the military to pray for divine deliverance ala the original Kamikaze (KK) winds, when the Mongol invasion attempts of Kublai Khan were defeated.[7]

Training: Instilling The Spirit

Ohnishi's call to the pilots brought immediate response: he chose twenty four veteran pilots and selected young, newly married Lieutenant Yukio Seki to be the leader (more on Seki later). The unit was dubbed Unit Shinpu.[8] As experienced pilots they were given but seven days of specialized training (two days for take off procedure, two days for formation flying, three days on how to approach and hit the ship) and then they were rushed from their Formosa training base to the Philippines.

As 1944 waned into 1945, and with the apparently unstoppable U.S. naval attacks moving north from the Philippines to the Ryukyus, Japan began to scour the nation's high school ranks for KK volunteers. Now 16, 17, and 18 year old youngsters were being recruited. Their training was hurried, minimal and often brutal. Training lasted about six months for these young neophytes. Some hardly mastered the intricacies of take off, formation flying, attack procedures, and landing. In order to toughen up the youngsters, they were made to run in the cold of winter and were beaten by older NCOs across their posteriors with baseball bats or wooden slats as they ran. The sergeants proclaimed: "Inferiors in rank should be treated like animals" (Many times NCOs were looked down upon by the officers). "NCOs knew this and this unjust prejudice stirred up their bile and this led them to take revenge."[9]

Kamikaze Psychology and Philosophy

In analyzing why Japanese youth unhesitatingly stepped forth to become Kamikaze pilots and to meet death, one must examine the following psychological and philosophical reasons:

• **Bushido**: This is the samurai code. It taught all Japanese from birth the principles of honor, courage, loyalty, the ability to endure pain, self sacrifice, reverence for the emperor and contempt of death. The principles of the Bushido Code had been given a more political interpretation and made an integral part of the national ideology. All had been indoctrinated with the idea that to die for the emperor was the most glorious event of their lives. Honor: "Do not attach too much to life—a human being who has lost his self respect through clinging too tenaciously to life is without honor," was reflected by one volunteer in his final letter.[10]

• **Religious Principles:** Some Japanese youth were imbued with strong religious motives be they Shintoist, Buddhist, Confucianist, or reverential of their ancient family heritage. Patriotic duty was not foremost, but their religious convictions made the idea of self sacrifice a method of attaining spiritual elevation thereby permitting them to join their venerated ancestors. These volunteers were also inspired by pride and looked upon the kamikaze pilots as role models for the entire nation. They were inspired by stories of the KK pilots' accomplishments and did not want to hesitate, for the KKs were doing noble deeds that covered them with glory and they were looked upon as legendary heroes.

• **Martial Tradition:** Some of the youths were steeped in the martial tradition since boyhood. These were your spontaneous heroes. Many were from the aristocracy or from the lower middle class families of samurai lineage who were particularly devoted to militarism. To be a KK pilot was a matter of patriotic duty, and death was tacitly accepted as a part of defending the emperor and nation. These men were the early volunteers and some had even crashed their planes into enemy planes and targets even before the formal call for KK volunteers.

• **"Freethinkers"/Military Strategists:** These were men who volunteered for less subjective reasons. They judged their kamikaze attacks in logical fashion: how effective was the tactic militarily; did the crash dive aid in the defeat of the enemy? Was it all worth while? Suicide was not looked upon as a self satisfying, final act. They were freethinkers in contrast to the others in that they were strongly affected in their thinking by logical analysis, not by patriotic fanaticism or religious glorification.

• **Morality/Tradition of Avoiding Haji:** The Japanese moral code held that voluntary death was better than living in shame. Unlike western beliefs, suicide was considered an honorable act. To die bravely was to avoid bringing shame to one's self and one's family members. Japanese, from early childhood, were continuously taught and reminded "never cause *haji* (shame) to the family)."

• **Philosophy of Obedience, Docility, Rejection of Individualism:** Japan exploited Western science and technology in order to advance her military goals. Through education, propaganda, and her state religion (Shinto), her leaders rejected all thoughts of individualism revered in the West. Materialism and nihilism were anathema to the Japanese, for those thoughts would disaffirm Japan's principles of obedience and docility. Obedience, docility, loyalty to and reverence of the throne, and military tradition engendered a widespread will to work and die for the good of the nation.

The Shinpu At The Leyte Gulf Operation

As noted earlier Lieutenant Seki led the first group of Kamikaze pilots. The *Tokubetsu Tokko Tai* (KK), also called Unit Shinpu,[11] received special training for seven days, then were ordered to commence the attacks. It was the 21st of October, 1944, when

Seki and three other KK pilots took off from Luzon to hit the American fleet at Leyte Gulf.[12] These were pilots who had volunteered, some had even fought for the opportunity to die for the emperor. They had all been indoctrinated from childhood that the most glorious thing was to die for the emperor so that their soul would be enshrined forever in the nation's national shrine of Yasukuni Jinja in Tokyo.

Prior to their departure Vice Admiral Takijiro Ohnishi gathered and addressed them:

> You are already gods without earthly desires. But one thing you want to know is that your crash dive is not in vain. Regrettably we will not be able to tell you the results. But I shall watch your efforts to the end and report your deeds to the throne. You may all rest assured on this point.[12]

The first flight ended in frustration. The pilots could not sight any enemy ships. One can imagine the emotional and psychological letdown. They had pumped themselves into a super state of mind-control only to face failure. The same thing occurred four days straight until the fifth day running. On the 25th of October, Seki and another pilot rammed into the baby carrier, *Saint Lo,* and sank it. Three other small carriers were hit. Immediately, Ohnishi, at his headquarters, made exaggerated claims: one carrier, one cruiser sunk; three other carriers heavily damaged. He trumpeted: "While the Imperial Naval fleet was being demolished in Leyte Gulf, single men in frail crafts against whole fleets is the miracle that Japan can boast of!"

Soon, Ohnishi convinced the Imperial Naval Command in Tokyo that the Special Attack Corps (KK) had to be expanded, and Tokyo rewarded him with 150 KK planes. These were sent to Taiwan to support the Philippine defense, and training bases were set up simultaneously in Taiwan.

By January, 1945, as the Philippines fighting shifted to the main island of Luzon, the KKs were proving their value. Furious attacks rained upon the U.S. fleet, and the battleship *New Mexico,* the cruiser *Louisville,* the destroyer *Walkde,* escort carriers *Manila*

Bay and HMAS *Australia*, and seven other ships were hit and damaged severely. Also, the carrier *Ommaney Bay* and the mine sweeper *Long* were sunk, with over a hundred persons killed. In the case of the carriers, many of the leading officers in the bridge area became flaming torches as the KK planes wrapped themselves around the bridge tower, having missed the side and the deck.

The Kamikaze In The Okinawa Operation

The Ohka (Baka Bomb): It was in the Battle of Okinawa, commencing 1 April, 1945, that the KKs consummated their most lethal frenzy. It was in this last battle that the Japanese introduced the Ohka (Cherry Blossom) bomb.[13] The Ohka was a glider drone with a sixteen foot wingspan and twenty foot body. Its nose was filled with 2,646 pounds of TNT. The KK pilot lowered himself into the cockpit of the Ohka drone which was tucked into the bomb bay of the twin engine Mitsubishi Betty bomber, and as the bomber neared the target area (twenty to thirty miles away) the Ohka was released on signal. Using rockets and gliding techniques it attained an amazing speed of 576 MPH.

    The results from the Japanese standpoint were horrible: of 800 bombs manufactured, only fifty reached the battle site, and of those only three exploded on target. Many of the planes carrying gliders—the Bettys—were shot down by the U.S. pilots since, because they were burdened, could travel less than 200 MPH. U.S. defenders jokingly called them the "BAKA (stupid) Bomb." Yet, the courage of the KK pilots was exceptional and unchallenged.

Operation Kikusui (Floating Chrysanthemum: The Battle of Okinawa was designed by the Japanese as a tropical Stalingrad. Lieutenant General Mitsuru Ushijima, who commanded the 32nd Imperial Japanese Army of 100,000 men, heavily fortified the lower one third of Okinawa. Okinawa is approximately 300 miles south of Kyushu and is sixty miles long and two to eighteen miles wide. Ushijima wanted Okinawa to be a massive sponge to absorb

American blood, ships and aircraft.

The Kikusui plan was to have the 32nd Army hold the U.S. land forces at bay while the Japanese navy was to demolish the American navy. The giant, 72,908 ton battleship *Yamato*, the cruiser *Yahagi*, and eight destroyers (the IJN was down to these ships only by this time), having enough fuel for only a one way trip to Okinawa, left the Inland Sea on 6 April, 1945. This was truly a suicidal mission too, for the two capital ships were to run themselves aground on the southern beaches and fire their big guns against the invading American ground troops.[14] The KKs from Kyushu and Okinawa were then to hurtle into the American ships at Okinawa. An American sailor reported:

> The deck near my gun mount was covered with blood, guts, brains, scalps, hearts, arms, etc., from the Jap pilots. They had to put the hose on to wash the blood off the deck. The deck ran red with blood. . . . One of the fellows had a scalp, it looked like you skinned an animal. The hair was black, but very short, and the color of the skin was yellow, real Japanese. . . . I do not think he was very old. I picked up a tin pie plate with a tongue on it. The pilot's tooth mark was into it very deep. It was very big and long, it looked like part of his tonsils were attached to it. . . . . This was the first time I ever saw a person's brains. What a mess. . . .[15]

In one 24-hour period, 6-7 April, 1945, 355 KKs and 350 conventional planes attacked the U.S. fleet at Okinawa. Yet the whole plan was suicidal and doomed to failure. Japan had overestimated her KK prowess, accuracy and effectiveness. The *Yamato* and *Yahagi*, along with four destroyers, never got to Okinawa—for without air cover they were easy victims of our marauding airplanes and submarines. Both were sunk one hundred miles south of Kyushu on 7 April, 1945. With but four destroyers left, the once proud and mighty Imperial Japanese Navy was no more.

Results—The Box-score: The following are the results of the Kamikaze attacks during the Pacific War:

U.S. Losses:
- Ships sunk: 34
- Ships damaged: 288
- KIA: 12,000 (4,000 were USN, 80% due to KK action)
- Lieutenant General Simon B. Buckner, commander of 10th U.S. Army on Okinawa, killed in action

Japanese Losses:
- KK pilots, planes and other aircraft destroyed: 9,228
- Japan lost ll0,000 KIA during Okinawa campaign
- 10,000 troops were captured (POWs)
- Lieutenant General Ushijima (Commanding General) and Lieutenant General Cho (Deputy Commanding General) of 32nd Imperial Japanese Army in Okinawa committed seppuku

Conclusion

This essay has focused on the issue concerning the motives of Japanese youth in volunteering for death. What urged them and prompted these youths to step forth unhesitatingly to become Japan's most bizarre World War II weapon? Without a doubt one can pinpoint their motivation to Japan's traditions and heritage. The Japanese mentality and patriotism that affected her people was deep-seated and rooted in her past—the deification of the motherland and her warriors. Japan's history is replete with the exploitation of the best of western technology, adapting what she needed for her immediate national goals, but rejecting "fanciful" western democratic ideals. Through propaganda, education and her Shinto religion, Japan's peoples were taught to maintain ancient beliefs and attitudes.

We, in the west, cannot accept the principle of suicide as a military weapon. Yet, upon serious reflection, one cannot help but consider the praiseworthy virtues of the Kamikaze volunteers. One cannot be insensitive and sneer at their virtues of courage, self-sacrifice, and determination.

We do not defend the Kamikaze phenomenon; the intention here is to shed some light on why these youths of Japan committed suicide. Suicides to be attributed not to a frenzied collective insanity but more to the logical result of a whole national psychology and culture reacting to the impending invasion of Japan. Yes, the Kamikaze pilots' sacrifices came to naught. But in line with their ancient past they stood out in the human virtues of courage, selflessness, and resolution.[16]

Notes

1. In the Battle of the Philippines Sea, the Japanese lost over 400 planes on 19 June, 1944. This precipitated the creation of the Tokubetsu Tokko Tai (Kamikaze unit, known as Unit Shinpu).

2. For a graphic description see "The Capital In Flames—Tokyo During The War Years," *The East*, 2 June, 1987, Vol. 23, No. 2, pp. 48-50.

3. Vice Admiral Takijiro Ohnishi, Vice Admiral Matome Ugaki, Captain Eiichiro Jyo.

4. Denis Warner, p. 71.

5. Reference "Turkey Shoot," where 476 planes were shot down by U.S. pilots, 19-21 June, 1944 (Leckie, p. 131).

6. Millot, p.24.

7. 1274 A.D. and 1281 A.D.

8. The Japanese reading of the kanji characters would be "*Kamikaze*." The Chinese reading of these characters, as phoneticized by the Japanese, is "*Shinpu*."

9. Nagatsuka, p. 80.

10. Nagatsuka, p. 80.

11. Newly married Lieutenant Yukio Seki was personally chosen by Admiral Ohnishi.

12. Seki and his Kamikaze companions took off after taking part in the traditional final ceremony. They toasted the emperor by downing three jiggers of water—the usual osake (rice wine) was not available that day—and with three *"banzais"* voiced by all they departed.

13. *Illustrated World War II Encyclopedia*, pp. 2473-2479.

14. The super battleship *Yamato* and her sister ships *Musashi* and *Shinano* were armed with massive 18.1 inch guns. The *Shinano* was converted into a carrier midway into the war.

15. Seaman 1st Class James Fahey, in E. Jablonski's *Wings Of Fire,* p.196.

16. *Divine Thunder*, p.233.

Selected Bibliography

Born To Die, Tr. by Nobuo Asahi and the Japan Tech Co., Hagoromo Society, The Cherry Blossom Squadrons (Ohara Publications, Inc., 1973).

Ienaga, Saburo, *The Pacific War 1931-1945* (New York, NY: Pantheon Books, 1968).

Illustrated World War II, Vol. 8 (New York, NY: H. S. Stuttman, Inc., 1978).

Ito, Masanori, Roger Pineau and Andrew Kuroda, *The End Of The Imperial Japanese Navy* (New York, NY: W.W. Norton, 1984).

Jablonski, Edward, *Wings Of Fire* (Garden City, NY: Doubleday and Co., 1972).

Kuwahara, Yasuo, and Gordon T. Allred, *Kamikaze* (New York NY: Ballantine Books, 1957).

Leckie, Robert, *The Story Of World War II* (New York, NY: Random House, 1964).

Naito, Hatsuho, *Thunder Gods: The Kamikaze Pilots Tell Their Story* (Tokyo, Japan: Kodansha, Inc., 1982).

Nagatsuka, Ryuji, *I Was A Kamikaze* (London, England: Abelard Schuman Ltd., 1973).

O'Neill, Richard, *Suicide Squads World War Ii* (New York, NY: St. Martin's Press, 1981).

Sakai, Saburo, Fred Saito and Martin Caidin, *Samurai!* (Annapolis, MD: Naval Institute Press, 1957).

The Japanese Navy In World War II (Annapolis, MD: United States Naval Institute, 1971).

Warner, Dennis, Peggy Warner and Sadao Seno, *The Sacred Warriors: Japan's Suicide Legions* (New York, NY: Van Nostrand Reinhold Co., 1982).

Topor, Ed, "Kamikaze, Death From The Sky," (MPI Home Video, 1989).

CHAPTER FIVE

JAPAN IN WAR AND PEACE: YESTERDAY'S ENEMY, TODAY'S FRIEND

Introduction

Amerca's World War II books, reports, essays and reflections are replete with our WWII planning, moves, emotions, and attitudes[1] as viewed from the American and western perspective. As a long time teacher of WWII history, I have often felt that my students were being denied the Japanese side of the story, and so I decided to go to Japan during my 1989 sabbatical. After extended correspondence with prospective Japanese WWII veterans and organizations, I traveled throughout central, western, and southern Japan to interview Japanese veterans in Tokyo, Osaka, Kyoto, Nara, Okayama, Izumo, Hiroshima, Fukiya, Nagasaki, and Okinawa. In an intense and busy month I interviewed and conversed with over fifty veterans.

Japanese, as many Americans have experienced, are quite reluctant to confer with strangers about their past, particularly about a war that they initiated against us. The fact, however, that I spoke and conducted the interviews in Japanese softened their resistance, relaxed them, and eventually became the elixir that triggered long ago memories. I could sense their feelings, note their attitudes and emotions as they responded eagerly to my questions.

Interviews

All interviews were taped, with the approval of each veteran, and were guided by a written series of questions that were versed in English and Japanese. After noting the individual data (name, rank, branch of service, date of entry into service, location of unit, combat dates, areas of operation, etc.), I then posed the following major questions:

- What were your thoughts when you first learned of Japan's attack on Pearl Harbor?

- What were you doing then: occupation, civilian status, societal status?

- What were your feelings when you received your personal national flag from your neighbors and friends (*Nishoki/Hinomaru*)?

- Briefly describe your service training.

- Describe your combat experiences: the enemy units opposing you, your unit's preparation for battle, the results, the chain of command, commander and mission of unit.

- What were your feelings as you prepared for combat, as the battle progressed, and as the battle ended?

- Where were you and what were your feelings when you learned about the atom bombings of Hiroshima and Nagasaki?

- Describe your feelings when you learned that Japan had lost the war and that you were to turn in your arms and surrender.

- Describe your feelings as you returned to Japan and viewed its destruction.

- What were your impressions when the U.S.A. sent in its troops to occupy Japan?

- What are your present views concerning U.S.-Japan relations?

In contacting individuals who were past members of the Imperial Japanese armed forces I searched for and used all resources available to me.[2] Since the location and setting was crucial, I made sure that every interview location was the choice of the interviewee and that a private setting was assured.[3]

When they entered service the veterans were within the age range of 17 to 38 years. Those in their thirties were usually draftees and saw combat in the South Pacific and China. The 17 to 24 year olds received their basic training as members of the High School Military Training Corps. Pilots and the officers received not only the HSMTC training but graduated into the *Yobi Shikan Gakko* (Officer Candidate School). Training of the Japanese soldier was intense and often brutal in contrast to western training methods. Salutes were mandatory among all ranks with privates, flight cadets and officer candidates undergoing constant harassment, bodily punches and even blows across their buttocks, to "toughen them up," as one pilot remarked. Cold showers were the rule, even in winter, and all training continued from dawn to dusk. One veteran remarked, "Today's young wouldn't be able to do it—they're too soft!"[4]

Pearl Harbor

The veteran's reflections concerning the Pearl Harbor attack proved interesting. Invariably their response would begin, "Do you really want to know? I'll tell you—it was a feeling of '*Yo Yatta*' (Good Work, we gave it to 'em')." Ensign Fujita who flew in the attack and reportedly shot down two U.S. planes was subdued in his remarks, saying,

I did not know what I was training for except that I felt it
must be for a large operation. We did not know what our
attack target would be until a few days prior to December
7th. Then I became excited and I was prepared to die. I
flew in the second wave and took off from the carrier
Akagi and fought over Pearl Harbor and Kaneohe Naval
Air Station. The anti-aircraft fire was coming at us hot
and heavy then. I remember my squadron leader signaling
to me that his plane was hit and he would be crash diving
into Kaneohe Naval Air Station. I saw him dive towards
the hangars but he did not make it and crashed into the
runway instead. Even I barely made it to the Akagi. When
I finally landed on the carrier a part from my engine (a
cylinder) fell on the deck. I was truly lucky![5]

Hiroshima

The Hiroshima veteran's interview was the most graphic:

I was having breakfast with my mother at Takahata-Yama
about thirty kilometers south of Hiroshima on 6 August. It
was about 0800 and I glanced through the window which
faced Hiroshima. Soon thereafter, a strong flash came
through—then a horrible explosion and shock wave followed, shaking our walls and the house nearly collapsed.
Then I saw a double storied plume and round cloud-burst,
first pink, then black . . . I immediately called my commander and he suggested that I take my mother home and
then report for duty at Kure . . . it was about eleven hundred hours as our train coursed its way slowly through
devastated Hiroshima, stopping constantly to pick up surviving derelicts. As people came through the train, some
had eyes hanging out of their eye sockets and some had
facial skin peeling off in globs. One person had one side
of his face completely skinned—it had been seared white
by the intense heat and was bleeding profusely. I tried to
help some victims climb on the slow moving train and as
I pulled on their arms their skin peeled off. Women had
the design of their *mompei* [war time blouse and pants]
seared into their bodies. I shall never forget this horrible
scene—it's been over forty years.[6]

Okinawa

The *Nishoki/Hinomaru*, (Individual battle flags, often wrapped around the stomachs of the soldiers) was usually presented to each serviceman by friends and relatives at a *sayonara* (good-bye) party. The Okinawa interviews were held at a *sushi-sake* beer party given by the grateful son of a deceased Okinawa veteran. Asato Nobuo, the son, lost his father in the battle for Mindanao Island, Philippines, in June, 1945.[7]

A White Bear Lake, Minnesota, former U.S. Army officer, Lt. Rex Campbell, after a fire-fight, took Asato's flag which had been wrapped around his torso. Through the many years Campbell had stored Asato's and other captured flags in his attic until 1987, when he asked the author to help in locating the bereaved family so that the

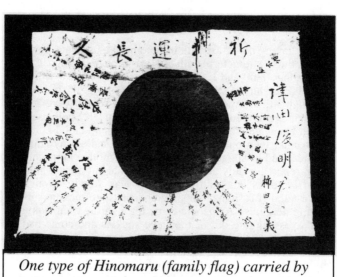

One type of Hinomaru (family flag) carried by individual servicemen of Japan

flag could be returned. After many months' search and with the aid of Japanese consular personnel, the Asato family was identified as the surviving kin and the flag was returned to the victim's son, Asato Nobuo. The flag, to the Japanese, is considered to be the spirit and soul of the individual soldier. The Asatos were overjoyed to have their father's personal flag, an important war memento, come back to the family. Throughout the interviews of the evening the flag was displayed in an auspicious position on the wall of the room.

The Japanese In Combat

In probing the inner thoughts of the Japanese servicemen in combat, the Japanese veterans were like American combatants.[8] They were scared at the outset but as the bullets and explosions rocketed around them, training and survival reactions took over. Veteran Norikazu Inouye remarked, "Our minds were completely filled with our duties and we were very afraid as soon as the bullets came at us; but when our companions fought back, we too, did our best." Veteran Adachi said,

> "We were being heavily bombed, we lost heavily and I saw two of my companions die before me—all Kure was burning. I was not afraid during the battle—I was so busy fighting that I had no time to fear. Those that had time, had time to be afraid; some even hid behind curtains—it was after the battle that I was shaking with fear."[9]

Suffering and intense hardships ruled the very existence of the Japanese servicemen, from frigid Siberia to the tropical south. Yet, national pride, discipline, and the hope of having their souls enshrined forever at Yasukuni Jinja[10] inspired many to fight to their utmost.

Matsuhiro Higa, captured in Siberia, said: "We were given one loaf of black bread a day to share among fourteen POWs. Arguments ensued concerning the size of each slice and so we had to make a crude scale . . ." Shuji Shibata, fighting on Okinawa, said:

> We were outnumbered and out-gunned so we fled into the mountains. Soon, we were driven to eat snakes, roots, flower buds, palm tree hearts, rodents, wild pigs, and garbage left by U.S. forces. Some could not struggle any more; they gave up hope and committed suicide by mouthing their rifles and pulling the trigger with their toes.

Ankichi Miyagi served in Mindanao, Philippines, and commented:

> Some of us were without weapons except for hand made bamboo spears, since we had fled hurriedly into the jungle. I lived three months in the jungle. Then Japanese MPs came and forced us to help the artillery troops wheel their big guns. They told us we were expendable and that we would have our spirits enshrined at Yasukuni.[11]

Hiroshima, Nagasaki Bombings

Most of the troops heard of the bombing of Hiroshima and Nagasaki through controlled military broadcasts, newspapers, or pamphlets and leaflets dropped by U.S. bomber crews. They were referred to as special bombs and, as they remarked, "We were not aware of the total destructive power of the A-Bombs until the war had officially ended. Then our reaction was one of '*Shikata-ga-nai*' (it can't be helped). War is war and we were total fools to think that our impoverished nation could defeat a rich, large and powerful country like the United States."[12]

End of the War
and Return Home

Without a doubt the Japanese veterans, returning home, were overjoyed. A Siberian veteran recounted, "Most of us had been captured a few days prior to the fall of Manchuria to the Russians in the waning days of the war [15 August, 1945 was the official end of World War II]. We did not return until 1948, and as my ship entered Maizuru harbor and as we saw our national flag, tears rolled down our cheeks and loud cheers of "*Banzai*" echoed throughout the ship and port."[13]

Even more poignant and heart rending were the reactions of those from Okinawa. Their island homes had been destroyed and over 150,000 civilians had become casualties during the horrendous Battle of Okinawa (1 April - 22 July, 1945.)[14] They commented, "When I returned to Maizuru from Siberia I heard that Okinawa had been totally destroyed and that all her people had been killed. But when I returned to Okinawa and saw that there were people in my homeland I was overjoyed."[15]

Yeiharu Nakamura recorded these stirring words:

> I did not receive any training when I was drafted on Okinawa because the Americans invaded the following day, 1 April, 1945. I was outfitted with only a bamboo spear and a shovel. Despite our hard fighting and true spirit we lost and I became a POW. I felt bad that Okinawa did not save Hiroshima. . . . Later, I wrote a 500 page monograph on Okinawa's destruction and surrender. I felt that we can beat the odds if we *gambare* [don't give up, persevere] and worked hard for Okinawa's future. I wanted the young of Okinawa to read my thoughts. Today, I feel we, as Japanese, should work equally hard to keep the future of Japan bright. I feel very bad that we still have the U.S. military in Okinawa.[16]

A veteran soldier who fought in Okinawa added these sympathetic words about the people of Okinawa.

> "The people of Okinawa were the real sufferers of all Japan. Other Japanese have no idea how much these people suffered. All Japanese owe them a great measure of respect and gratitude for all the hard servitude and suffering that they went through. I urge everyone I meet to visit Okinawa and visit the Kenji-no-To and the Himeyuri-no-To memorial sites and appreciate the courage, discipline and sacrifices these young people showed in their desperate attempt to help the Japanese army and their country."[17]

When hostilities ended on 15 August, 1945, all the veterans were jubilant and had visions of returning to their homes immediately. That was not to be for those in overseas areas. Some of the Siberian veterans did not return until the mid-fifties and those in the Philippines were grateful that they were POWs of the Americans and not the Filipinos. A grateful veteran said,

I surrendered to the Americans on 9 September, 1945. I was greatly impressed with the size and height of the U.S. troops. I was
equally surprised to see Nisei (Japanese American) soldiers in the
U.S. Army. They could speak Japanese and they stopped the
Filipino civilians and soldiers from abusing us. They were beating
us with bamboo sticks and throwing stones at us as they yelled
Japan—Bakayaro, Dorobo, Patai! [Japan — You stupid beast, rob-
ber, you die!]. I am grateful to the Nisei soldiers and thought, truly,
America must be a great country to have even those with Japanese
ancestry serve in their army.[18]

When they returned to Japan and came into contact with
American Occupation troops, reactions generally differed. One ex-
pilot said, "I flew with the first U.S. pilots to use our airdrome near
Maizuru to familiarize them with Japan's air procedures. At first I
felt nothing but disgust in having lost to the Americans, but soon, as
I flew with them, we became great friends and I wondered why we
ever fought against such good and kindly people."[19]

Another remarked, "It was a natural thing for our country to
be occupied—we lost, yet, today, I realize that our good life and
standing was because of MacArthur's fair occupation policy. He
saved us from the Russians!"[20]

Two others lamented in the following fashion. "I had a feeling of disgust when I saw our Japanese girls together with U.S. soldiers." The other complained, "Our home was taken over and occupied by a U.S. Army colonel and he made a mess of it so I did not
have a good feeling for the U.S. Occupation forces."[21]

Conclusion

These interviews are by no means conclusive concerning
experiences of all of Japan's war veterans, but they are representative
of an older generation with deep, intense feelings of service and allegiance to the emperor and the nation. No interviewee decried the
imperial system; rather, they praised the emperor and considered him

to be the savior of Japan and her national polity. They are proud of being Japanese and that they had fought hard for their country. Yet, to a man, having seen the death and destruction of war, they question whether Japan had to go to war. Today, in their retirement years, they admit that war is foolish, and in the light of Japan's phenomenal rise in economic power, superhuman efforts should be harnessed to safe-guard peace. "War does not solve anything," they say.

In many ways they are like America's veterans. They are politically and socially conservative. They decry the lack of nation-al consciousness, the new materialistic values and the minimizing of Japan's traditional values among many of Japan's modern youths. True, they have not had any flag burning but they are greatly con-cerned about Japan's aging population being cared for by govern-mental agencies rather than by their sons and daughters. They abhor and worry about the modern generation's diminishing respect for fil-ial piety.

In sum, Japan's fierce warriors of World War II have mel-lowed like our own veterans. They were impressively sincere in their remarks to me and emphasized that it would be the greatest of tragedies to allow economic or political differences to be a catalyst to any form of renewed enmity by either country towards the other. They were outspoken in their remarks that America and Japan remain friends forever and all cultural, social, and educational efforts be maximized to bring about better U.S.-Japan relations. The veterans of Japan have extended their hands of friendship to all Americans and as Ensign Sakamaki Kazuo, our first Japanese POW has written, "Yesterday's enemy is today's friend!"[22]

End Notes

1. Too often the Japanese were referred to as "yellow-bellied mon-sters," "Japs," "Nips," etc. (Manchester, p. 61).

2. This included the Japanese Veterans Association, past Japanese students, faculty and visitors at Century College, American and Japanese contacts and personal friends living in Japan, American

mission churches in Japan, past AFS and Rotary Club exchange students, ESL (English as a Second Language) faculty and administrators in Japan, and chance contacts uncovered during the interviews or while conversing during my sojourn in Japan.

3. Interviews were conducted in institutional buildings (offices or empty classrooms) such as veterans halls, colleges, high schools, factories, or corporate offices. Some individuals were interviewed in restaurants and bars. Fascinating interviews were conducted with a dozen veterans in a home in Okinawa. They had the family's nisho-ki (battle flag) proudly displayed on the wall, and low tables were laden with a superb feast. Another interesting interview was held at a local bar in Izumo when a bar patron excitedly recounted his war experiences upon hearing of my WWII Japan project.

4. Masazumi Kamashita, a Japan Army Air Force pilot who also received kamikaze training and would have perished had the war lasted longer (Kuwahara and Allred, pp. 35-40).

5. Ensign Iyuzo Fujita.

6. Tsutomu Adachi, a naval ensign, was stationed at Kure and had liberty for a few days eighteen miles south of Hiroshima when the A-Bomb exploded, 6 August, 1945.

7. Nobuo Asato's home was the scene of the party and interviews with the Japanese veterans of Okinawa.

8. Pearl Harbor survivor Robert Hudson reported that he was astounded and surprised beyond his wits, but when the machine gun bullets began whizzing around him he forgot all his fears and began fighting back from his ship.

9. Interviews of Norikazu Inouye and Tsutomu Adachi.

10. Japan's hallowed national shrine located in Tokyo.

11. Interviews with Matsuhiro Higa, Shuji Shibata and Ankichi Miyagi.

12. Interviews with Takaichi Eda, Takeo Iiguni, Tsutomu Adachi, Shizuo Omoto and Mitsuo Ishitobi.

13. Interview with Fumio Goto.
14. Ota, p. 249.

15. Interview with Matsuhiro Higa.

16. Interview with Yeiharu Nakamura.

17. Interview with Shibata, Shuji, who was a lieutenant in the Battle of Okinawa. The Kenji-no-To and Himeyuri-no-To memorialize over 150 high school students who were blasted by the Americans in their cave sites as they aided the Imperial Japanese Army working as message center runners or as nurses' aides.

18. Interview with Shizuo Omoto.

19. Interview with Takashi Matsumura.

20. Interview with Mitsuo Ishitobi.

21. Interview with Dr. Morita, T. and Fukuma, Hiroshi.

22. Sakamaki, Kazuo, captain of a midget submarinewho was captured in an abortive attempt to enter Pearl Harbor and torpedo U.S. capital ships on 7 December, 1941. Quoted from Sakamaki's letter to Donald B. Haynie, First Shot Naval Vets, St. Paul, Minnesota, 10 February 1969.

Bibliography

Ota, Masahide: *The Battle of Okinawa,* Tokyo, Kume Publishing, 1984, p. 249.

Kuwahara, Yasuo, and Gordon T. Allred, *Kamikaze*, (New York NY: Ballantine Books, 1957).

CHAPTER SIX

CHIUNE (SEMPO) SUGIHARA: JAPAN'S OSKAR SCHINDLER

Introduction

Moviegoers throughout the world are familiar with Steven Spielberg's movie "Schindler's List," a dramatic film of a greedy Nazi industrialist who was able to save 1,200 Jews through personal connections to the Nazi party and his aggressive chutzpa.[1] A more remarkable feat of a person saving thousands of persecuted Jews is the World War II story of Chiune (Sempo) Sugihara. Sugihara, with compassion, sympathy, persistence and bravery was able to give continued life to 6000 to 8,000 Jews, and some say as many as 40,000 if one were to count the descendants of the Jews he saved.[2]

The purpose of this essay is to relate and inform everyone of the amazing yet sad tale of one man who listened to cries for help, obeyed his conscience, stood firm on his moral convictions, and saved human beings rather than obey the fiat of a bureaucratic foreign ministry. This is the story of Chiune (Sempo) Sugihara.

Early Years

Sugihara was born on 1 January, 1900 in Yaotsu, Gifu Prefecture, located in central Japan. Chiune did exceedingly well in his earlier studies, graduating with honors. His father wanted Chiune to study medicine but Chiune was more a student of languages, concentrating in English, and purposely failed the Keio University Entrance Examination in 1917 after graduating from his high school. He enrolled at Waseda University, majoring in English literature in 1918. During the year, he happened upon a Foreign Ministry announcement concerning a competitive exam to study diplomacy. Intrigued and always desirous of world travel, Chiune Sugihara took and passed the exam with flying colors. He was then sent to Harbin (Manchuria) National University to study Russian.

By 1923 Sugihara had graduated with top honors and was appointed a clerk in the Harbin Japanese Embassy. His career as a foreign ministry diplomat was launched. From 1924 until 1934 he ascended steadily in diplomatic responsibilities concentrating on Northern Manchurian Railroad acquisitions, and as section chief of

Mr. Chiune Sugihara at his consul desk (photo courtesy of Mrs. Sugihara).

Russian and Planning. In 1934 the first sign of his humanitarian tendencies evolved when he resigned his Manchurian post, protesting the inhuman Japanese treatment of Chinese in Manchuria. Marrying Yukiko Kikuchi in 1935, he was then posted to Helsinki, Finland, and next appointed Consul in Kaunas, Lithuania, in 1939.[3]

Sugihara's Lifesaving Actions

It was in Kaunas that Sugihara showed his true mettle as an humanitarian. On 27 July, 1940, Consul Sugihara awakened to shouts outside his home in Kaunas. As he peeked out the window he noted hundreds of frightened, beleaguered men and women, some with babies in their arms or toddlers holding on to their parents' hands. Many were men who were bearded wearing caftans, and fur hats or yamulkas. "Those are Jews and they want you to save them by issuing transit visas to Japan and other points—they're fleeing from the German invasion of Poland," said one of their housekeepers.[4]

The only escape route fleeing the rampaging German army was an overland railroad trip through Russia to points beyond Japan. A few days earlier Chiune Sugihara, as the Japanese Consul in Kaunas, had issued transit visas to a few Jews to go through the USSR to Japan with final destination being Curacao, a Dutch island possession in the Caribbean Sea. The Jewish network spread the news that Consul Sugihara was issuing transit visas and this caused the hubbub in front of Sugihara's home whose first floor doubled as the consulate.

Sugihara requested the crowd to appoint five representatives and he would meet with them. One of the five was a young lawyer named Zorach Warhaftig and he recalls saying: "We are Jews escaping from the Nazis in Poland. There are no countries in Europe that we can flee to. We want to go to free countries by way of Japan with transit visas. If we do not leave here, they will kill us for sure. Please help us!"[5]

Sugihara's wife, Yukiko and their five year old son, Hiroki, saw the crowd outside and said to her husband "You must help them, no matter the orders from Tokyo." Chiune told Warhaftig and the other four representatives that he must contact the foreign ministry in Tokyo to receive instructions concerning their request for transit visas.

Tokyo cabled back instructions two days later; "You are not to issue transit visas to those people who do not have a designated destination." Sugihara cabled a second time explaining the life or death plight for the thousands of Jews who were now crowded in front of his home. He argued that the people would need twenty days to cross the Soviet Union and cross over the Sea of Japan from

Jewish refugees at gate of consulate, 1940 (Photo courtesy of Mrs. Sugihara).

Vladivostok and then have 30 days in Japan before going to their final destination — in total 50 days, for in that time the refugees would be able to locate a final destination. Again the reply from Tokyo was a firm "NO!"

Sugihara cabled a third time indicating the thousands of Jews in front of the Kaunas Consulate would all be massacred by the oncoming Nazi forces unless he issued them transit visas. Again a firm "NO!"

It was clear to Sugihara that he must follow his government's orders or follow his conscience. He consulted his wife Yukiko and son Hiroki. Both urged him to follow his conscience and save the Jews.[6] Sugihara had converted to Christianity (Greek Orthodox) during his study and assignment in Harbin, Manchuria, and he told his wife, "If I issue the transit visas I will be disobeying the Foreign Ministry and I will lose my job. And if I don't these Jews will die— I can't have that on my conscience. I must follow God's will."[6]

His wife Yukiko agreed and so Sempo announced to the crowd that he would issue transit visas. He asked Warhaftig to have the joyous people form a line. This was on 1 August, 1939. At first he asked them the standard questions: "Do you have enough money to buy a ticket across Russia?" "Do you have a final acceptable destination?" Warhaftig had obtained a written statement that Curacao did not require an entry visa so almost all blurted out "Curacao." Soon, however, Sempo realized that hundreds of the refugees had left Poland with only their shirts on their backs and in order to save them he had to hurry his writing and stamping process. He omitted the questions and began writing visas day and night, sometimes not even stopping for his meals. His wife continued to support him and gave him soothing massages on his back and writing hand and arm.

Sempo had run out of official forms so he began handwriting the visas—a most laborious process. His eyes were bloodshot and he gave serious thought to quitting but when he looked out at the sad, distraught, yet hopeful people, and with Yukiko's continued urging to save as many as he could, Sugihara continued his frantic pace of writing out the visas.

By the third week of August, Tokyo was frantically cabling him to cease writing out visas. Yokohama and Kobe were now being flooded by the Jewish refugees. Chiune Sugihara paid no mind to the cables and continued writing. It was now the end of August and Soviet authorities ordered Japan to shut down all their Lithuanian consulates. Tokyo ordered Sugihara to Berlin. Chiune gave up his residence and told the beseeching crowd that he will spend one night at a certain hotel and will write out visas from his hotel room. Thousands of hopeful Jews followed him all the way to the hotel where he continued his frenzied writing.

The next morning they followed him and his family to the train station where Sugihara continued to write visas and passed them to the waiting Jews from the train window. He then began signing only his name to blank sheets of paper that he tossed out to the Jews hoping that the Jews would be able to fill in the necessary documentary statements. One of the refugees yelled out as the train departed, "Sempo, we shall never forget you!" Years later Yukiko recalled that train depot scene with tears in her eyes. She composed a 31 syllable ode (tanka), *"Hashiri izuru ressha no mado ni sugarikuru Te ni watasaruru inochi no visa wa"* (From the window of the moving train, life saving visas were passed out to pleading outstretched hands).[7]

Each visa was applicable to a whole family and so the Japanese Foreign Ministry officials calculated at least 6,000 Jews had come to Japan on the basis of Sugihara's visas and thence moved to Shanghai, and Manchuria, China, or were allowed to stay in Japan. Many of the Jews then went to Israel, South Africa, South America, or the United States after the war. Recent Jewish scholars such as Boston University's Hillel Levin, pouring over the war time Japanese Foreign Ministry records, discovered a 31 page registry of Jewish names and so the estimate has been raised to a very probable 8,000 Jews who were saved by the great humanitarian Sugihara. Extending the total count to the descendants of these "saved" Jews, Sugihara was undoubtedly responsible in saving as many as 40,000 humans.[8]

Sugihara's Bitter Life
After Kaunas And in Postwar Japan

Sugihara was assigned consular duties in Berlin, Prague, Koenigsberg and suffered through a two year hitch in Bucharest, Rumania, during the war. When the Soviets rolled into Rumania he and his whole family were held by the Soviets in a POW camp for 16 months until December 1946 when all Japanese were ordered to return to Japan. The Sugiharas suffered another long and arduous trek, always concerned about food, clothing, safety and shelter until they finally made it back to Japan via Siberia in April 1947.[9]

When the Sugiharas finally returned they found Japan in devastation. Large buildings were burned or flattened by bombs. It was grim destruction all over. The people were in complete poverty, hunger, disease, cold—morale was practically zero. The Sugiharas finally settled in Fujisawa City, within a few hour's ride by train from Tokyo.

After three months of anxious waiting Chiune was summoned by the Vice Foreign Minister. Chiune was hopeful for an ambassadorship, having climbed the consular steps during the war. Unfortunately Sugihara was informed by Vice Foreign Minister Okazaki: "Turn in your resignation—we have no post available for you and we cannot take you under our wing." Later on, Mrs. Sugihara learned that Okazaki had been more direct, having said to Sempo, "It is because of that incident in Lithuania. We can no longer take you under our wing."[10]

Thoroughly depressed, yet knowing that he must make a living, Sempo tried everything to keep his family in food and daily necessities. He, at 47, was unemployable as a linguist. Sempo even tried selling light bulbs from door to door. In 1950 fortunes changed for the better when he was appointed manager of an Occupation Forces' Tokyo Post Exchange. His ability to speak English cinched the job.

The following year Sugihara obtained a job as manager of an American trading company in Tokyo and, taking advantage of his Russian language proficiency, they sent him to Moscow to manage their Moscow branch for the next 15 years. Chiune was separated from his family during the 15 years except for occasional visits back to Tokyo. He and his wife rarely spoke of their Kaunas experiences during this period, seemingly. For Chiune, this was a painful phase of his life that he wanted to forget.

Sempo Sugihara, We Shall Never Forget You

In 1967, the eldest son of Sempo, Hiroki Sugihara, received a message from Yehoshua Nishri, an Israeli Embassy official in Tokyo. He explained, "I want to see your father and I can't seem to trace him. The Japanese Foreign Ministry has not helped me at all. They tell me they can't locate him. I was able to contact you through the foreign ministry alumni network. Will you please help me and put me in touch with your father. I've been looking for your father for years. I could never forget the man that saved my life."[11]

Hiroki explained that his father was working in Moscow. Nishri then told Hiroki, "Tell him that Israel wants to honor him for what he did." When Hiroki contacted his father with the message, Sempo responded in his typical business-comes-first approach, "I'm too busy to go traveling to Israel to receive official thanks. Tell him that I only did what anyone else would do under the circumstances." In August, 1968, a tearful Nishri met and surprised Sempo with a yellowed visa that Sempo had given him in Kaunas. Thereupon, Nishri convinced Sempo to visit Israel in 1969 where official government parties and private survivors' celebrations were held in his honor.

Sempo was delighted to meet and renew friendships with those whom he had rescued: Zorach Warhaftig who had helped write Israel's Declaration of Independence and was then the Minister of

Chiune Sugihara with Zorach Warhaftig, Religious Minister of Israel—one of the Sugihara survivors, 1969 (Photo, courtesy of Mrs. Sugihara).

Religious Affairs; Josef Shimkin, who went to Shanghai and created a large trading firm; Igo Feldblum, a Haifa physician, and Nishri. Israel treated him as a national hero. An older couple who had been saved and considered themselves as "Sugihara's Jews" told his son, Nobuki, "your father saved us and now we have 30 grand-children." Another, Daniel Zoltek, of Toronto, Canada, said, "If it wasn't for

Sugihara I would be murdered in a burning oven—just like the rest of my family. I will never forget him as long as I live."[12] Samuel Minski, Farmington, Massachusetts, commented, "Everyone is talking about Schindler, but he used people as slave labor and made money off of them. I'm not minimizing what he did, but I feel that we are forgetting the people who did these acts for pure good. Mr. Sugihara didn't get any money for what he did and he suffered greatly for it. If it were not for his generosity and humanity I would not be here today.[13]

Honors Bestowed Upon Chiune (Sempo) Sugihara

In 1985 Israel honored Sugihara with the Yad Vashem Award (Righteous Among Nations), and a memorial park was inaugurated on Beit Shemesh Hill in Jerusalem in Sugihara's honor. This was not the end of recognition. Unfortunately, Sugihara died on 31 July 1986, in his sleep, after suffering several heart attacks. Jews from throughout the world sent cards and condolences to Mrs. Yukiko Sugihara, but the death was hardly noticed in Japan.

Belatedly, in 1991, Japan's Foreign Ministry apologized formally to Yukiko Sugihara for terminating Chiune Sugihara's diplomatic career in 1947. Japan was becoming aware of the brave humanitarian contributions of Sugihara, and the media (TV and press) rushed to cover the saga of Sugihara. Yukiko had published a best selling book about her husband's work entitled *Visas For Six Thousand Lives*.

In August 1991, Lithuania honored Sugihara by naming one of Kaunas' streets "Sugihara Street." The following year, in Sugihara's birthplace of Yaotsu, a beautiful memorial park called "Hill of Humanity" was dedicated in his honor and Jews as well as others came to eulogize his contributions to peace and humanity.[14]

The Nisei 522nd
Field Artillery Battalion

On 23 September 1994, a delegation of veterans from the 522nd Field Artillery Battalion (442nd RCT) along with Military Intelligence Service veterans, accompanied a contingent of "Sugihara's Jews" and their descendants to honor Chiune Sempo Sugihara at Yaotsu, Gifu Prefecture, the latter's birthplace. A hilltop at Yaotsu was dedicated as the "Hill of Humanity" which had been impressively landscaped to include a bronze bust of Sugihara. There representatives from the U.S. Consulate in Nagoya, the Japanese Foreign Ministry, Mrs. Yukiko Sugihara and her family, and survivors, made commemorative speeches in honor of Sugihara. Then three of the survivors, Marsha Leon, Jerry Milrod, and Solly Ganor laid wreaths at Sugihara's memorial bust. Ganor recalled being half buried in the snow at Dachau during the final days of the war and being miraculously rescued by members of the 522nd FAB—clearly heaven sent, according to Ganor—for his rescuers were once more ethnic Japanese.[15]

Sugihara's eldest son, Hiroki, has taken on the task of illumining the heroic accomplishments of his father, a man who followed his conscience and saved thousands of Jews, instead of obeying the dictates of a hide-bound government ministry. Hiroki has traveled the world to relate the story of one Japanese diplomat who, by his humanitarian actions, made a difference and contributed to world peace. This is the story of Chiune Sempo Sugihara, Japan's Oskar Schindler.

Notes

1. A Hebrew Yiddish colloquial term meaning shameless audacity, independence, brass (*Webster's New World Dictionary of American Language,*).

2. Tsukiyama, p. A-l.

3. Sugihara, p. 146.

4. Tracey, p.69.

5. Tsukiyama, p. A-10.

6. Tracey, p.76.

7. Tsukiyama, p. A-11.

8. Tsukiyama, p. A-11.

9. Tsukiyama, p. A-11.

10. Sugihara, pp. 108-109.

11. Tracey, pp. 73-74.

12. Tsukiyama, p. A-11.

13. Tsukiyama, p. A-11.

14. Sugihara, p. 147.

15. Lee, p. A-9.

References

Books:

Lee, Stacy, "Mission To Japan: The Unlikely Liberators," *The Hawaii Herald,* (Honolulu, Hawaii: Hochi Ltd., 1994).

Sugihara, Yukiko, *Visas For Life* (South San Francisco, CA: Edu-Com Plus, 1993).

_____, *Visas For Six Thousand People* (Tokyo, Japan: Taisho Publishing Company, 1991).

Tracy, David, "Visas For Life," *Reader's Digest* (Pleasanton, MD: 1994).

Tsukiyama, Ted, "Chiune Sempo Sugihara," *The Hawaii Herald,* (Honolulu, HA: Hochi Ltd., 1994).

Internet

"Japanese Schindler Honored For His Acts of Courage," http://burn.ucsd.edu/%7Earchive/riot-l/1995.Nov/0131.html

S'u g i h a r a , C h i u n e , "h t t p : / / c c 2 0 0 0 . k y o t o - su.ac.jp/information/famous,/sugiharac.html

"Son of Holocaust Hero Praises His Father's Action," http:/www.yale.edu/ydn/paper/4.15.96/4.15.96story no.BC.html

Audio-Visual Media

"Visas and Virtues," Cedar Grove Productions, P.O. box 29772, Los Angeles, CA 90029-0772.

CHAPTER SEVEN

THE JAPANESE-PERUVIANS

Introduction

Most Americans are familiar with the forced evacuation and incarceration of over 120,000 ethnic Japanese Americans into ten relocation camps located away from the Pacific coast. This essay concerns another perfidious action of our government during World War II, how the United States and Peruvian governments conspired and collaborated intimately, hand in glove, to remove all Japanese from Peru with the advent of World War II. The reasons? War, politics, economics, racism—all played their deviltry in this tragic experience. By the end of the war, 2,260 Japanese Latin Americans, over 90 percent being Japanese Peruvians, were arrested, in a few cases even kidnapped off the streets or from their homes, hauled into local jails, and subsequently shipped off to the United States, there to be imprisoned in Immigration and Naturalization Service Camps.[1]

Background

Japan's industrialization effort during the Meiji Period (1868-1912) caused her population to bulge. The pressure was particularly strong in the south and southwestern prefectures since in Japanese culture siblings of the first son could not inherit the father's properties. With the advent of prolonged droughts that visited the Inland Sea area during the 1880's and 90's this cultural norm forced the lesser members of many families to look overseas for resettlement.[2] Many of these early immigrants from Japan had flowed into Hawaii (from 1885 on) and the continental United States. However, with the Gentlemen's Agreement of 1907, the U.S. was summarily closed to Japanese labor.

Peru, on the other hand, needed laborers for her coastal sugar plantations. Chinese laborers, who had come to Peru as early as 1849, had proven difficult to work with in the fields, and by 1909 contract immigration for Chinese had ceased. Japanese laborers, on the other hand, had proven to be successful in the Hawaiian sugar plantations. The Peruvian government thereupon approved Japanese immigration.

The steamship *Sakura Maru* subsequently docked at the port of Callao on 3 April, 1899, with 790 emigrants from the Japanese prefectures of Okayama, Yamaguchi, Hiroshima, and Niigata—and by 1923 the number of Japanese had increased to 17,598. The Japanese-Peruvian people slowly increased until the advent of WWII, despite the fact that there were more Japanese leaving Peru than coming in. By 1942 the total had swelled to approximately 30,000, a third being Nisei.[3]

Originally the Japanese immigrants were laborers on the sugar haciendas but they soon tired of the rural peasant scenario and at the first opportunity moved into the urban areas. By 1940 over eighty percent lived in the Callao and Lima metropolitan areas. There they quickly assumed occupations characteristic of towns and cities. Many became barbers, grocers, shopkeepers, store owners, restaurateurs, wholesalers, importers, jewelers, contract laborers, building laborers, carpenters, plumbers, painters, etc.

As one might expect, the native Peruvians, especially business competitors and those who depended on store credit to exist, developed strong anti-Japanese attitudes. In rural areas Peruvians lamented that Japanese farmers controlled most of the fertile Chancay Valley and other coveted agricultural areas. The strong Japanese racial and cultural pride, and the diaspora-like togetherness of the Japanese, added much to the distrust and hatred of the Japanese in Peru.[4] Then too, Chinese immigrants who preceded the Japanese by half a century had left an active anti-Asian backlash in Peru.

Aftermath of Pearl Harbor Attack

Immediately after the Japanese attack on Pearl Harbor, rumors and half truths spawned ridiculous myths that fanned the anti-Japanese hatred in Peru. The most prevalent story was that all Japanese male youths were members of the Imperial Japanese Army Reserve Corps.

Peruvian law was at best vague concerning the rights of aliens to remain permanently within the country. The president of the country claimed the express authority to exclude aliens in-country when he ruled that "national security or public order" was threatened. The vulnerability of Japanese Peruvians was now clearly evident.

The first actions taken by Peru were to close all Japanese newspapers, and groups of three or more were forbidden. The United States thereupon became involved in this imbroglio through several developments:

- First, with the approval of Congress, by summer 1941 FBI Director J. Edgar Hoover posted several of his agents to "look into" and cooperate with Peruvian officials in pinpointing and removing potential Japanese-Peruvian spies and saboteurs.

- Second, U.S. Ambassador R. Henry Norweb enthusiastically offered "suggestions" and information on how to control Japanese Peruvians, based on the U.S. experience with the relocation of Japanese Americans then taking place in 1942.

- Third, Secretary John Emmerson, the only person in the state department's Latin America division fully qualified as a Japanese linguist, served twenty months in Peru from February 1942 to aid the Peruvians in locating and deporting Japanese Peruvians.[5]

- Fourth, Peruvian officials studied the deportation of all Panamanian Japanese by U.S. and Panama after Pearl Harbor as a model to be emulated.

U.S. interest in the Peruvian situation mounted as the Japanese military swept through China, Philippines, and Southeast Asia. Thousands of American civilians became prisoners of the Japanese Army and our government's intent was to attempt a trade of Japanese Peruvians and or Japanese Latin Americans (JLAs) in exchange for our captured civilians.[6]

Abduction, Transportation and Incarceration in the U.S.A.

With Peru being willing, nay anxious, to rid itself of all Japanese, and with the cooperation of the U.S. government, the decision was made to transfer the bulk of Japanese Peruvians for possible deportation, first to the U.S.A. and thence, eventually, to Japan.[7] Peru's government officials fanned the blaze of public hatred by declaring that "shop-keepers of Lima's Japanese Peruvians could set the city of Lima on fire overnight," and "restaurateurs could poison their customer's foods," and that "the U.S. had underestimated the Japanese in Peru and they urged all Japanese to be confined in concentration camps."[8]

From February, 1942, John Emmerson was busy listing all possible Japanese non-diplomatic personnel to be picked up by the Peruvian authorities. The major hitch was the lack of any shipping from Peru to the United States. The first ship, the *Etolin,* did not leave Callao until 5 April, 1942, yet hundreds of Japanese-Peruvians had been summarily locked up in the city jails. Truly, the months of

February, March, and April were hellish for them and resulted in widespread fear, uncertainty and wretchedness as they realized that the Peruvian and United States governments were targeting them without regard for their individual rights. Some were even kidnapped off the streets or out of their homes to fill the Peruvian police's assigned quota of Japanese.[9] Emmerson was later to admit that:

> As I look back on the Peruvian experience I am not proud to have been part of the Japanese operation. One steeled oneself against the heart break being inflicted on hundreds of innocent Japanese caught up in the war-generated hysteria that marked each of them a suspect. It is hard to justify our pulling them from their homes of years and herding them, whether born in Japan or Peru, onto ships bound for a strange land, where they would live in concentration camps under conditions which at best were difficult . . .[10]

The next ship to leave Peru and to pick up other Japanese Latin Americans was the *Arcadia*. The first ship anchored in San Francisco, where the passengers went by rail to Kenedy, Texas. The *Arcadia* and subsequent ships all went through the Panama Canal to New Orleans. From these ports the Japanese Peruvians were sent by rail to Kenedy or Seagoville and later on, to Crystal City, Texas. By the end of the war, over 2,000 persons were transported to the United States. No one had the right to refuse transshipment. All of their rights were quashed, their passports were confiscated and they were informed by the INS (Immigration and Naturalization Service) that they were "illegal aliens" in the United States awaiting expulsion and repatriation to Japan.

Early internees were all male and unaccompanied. They were housed in Camp Kenedy and Seagoville, Texas, and lesser groups were sent to Fort Missoula, Montana, and Santa Fe, New Mexico. Although most were from Peru, other Japanese Latin Americans from Panama, Costa Rica, Mexico, Ecuador, and Nicaragua, were also sent to INS operated camps in the United States.

Camp Life

As 1943 dawned, camp life in Kenedy and Seagoville became almost intolerable for the all-male internees, especially due to the humidity and other weather conditions. Also, the lack of privacy, the same faces and voices daily, the close and constant proximity of individuals—all tended to breed hatred and distrust of others. Secretiveness, jealousy, pettiness over trivia, scandal mongering, and argumentativeness became frequent, even among these ordinarily quiet, solemn, staid and sober Japanese Issei. The difficult pattern of living made even the dignified resort to rivalries and gang confrontations. Many developed hypochondria, imagining illness, to escape daily routines. These traits continued into life at Crystal City, Texas, where they were later to be transferred to join their families.

As had happened in the Japanese American experiences, camp life for the Japanese-Peruvians tended to weaken family ties; parental discipline suffered, especially due to parents being unable to control the children in the mess halls, social gatherings, or in public areas. Since the youth communicated in English or Spanish, fathers in particular felt that their traditional role as family head suffered and was being ignored. Many Issei became morose and quiescent and felt displaced. This trauma continued at Crystal City, too, as they were internees there until 1945.

Crystal City, Texas

As other ships became available the remaining family members were shipped to New Orleans, thence by rail to more spacious and livable quarters at Crystal City, Texas.[11] This INS camp soon became the nucleus of all INS camps, and, by war's end, over 3,300 internees, including a significant number of German and Japanese American families, were brought there. The Japanese American families were those whose family heads had demanded to be repatriated to their native Japan. They had given up on America!

Life at Crystal City, proclaimed these Japanese American

families, was much better than the ten concentration camps they had left, since they were now quartered in roomier cottages, triplexes, or duplexes, with cooking, bathing and toilet facilities.   English, Japanese, and German language schools were established and running smoothly by 1943. Youths were involved in student government, club and social activities, including a prom. They also participated in athletic competitions, in baseball, soccer, basketball, softball, ping pong, tennis, swimming, hiking, and many other non-academic outlets, such as the Boy Scouts and Allied Youth. These activities for the young made life at Crystal City fun and memorable.[12]

Early Repatriation

On 2 September, 1943, an exchange between the U.S. and Japan was made of 1,340 Japanese civilians for an equal number of American civilians. These Japanese departed from New York on *MS Gripsholm*. This was the second exchange. The first, in 1942, was comprised chiefly of diplomatic personnel. The U.S. government wanted the exchange system to continue, with 1,500 as the next shipment, and had as bait the Japanese Peruvians held in the INS camp at Crystal City.   In order to swell the number of Japanese Latin Americans, Attorney General Francis Biddle had already given approval for the internment of "283 persons in Chile, 130 in Bolivia, 92 in Paraguay, 23 in Uruguay, and 24 in Venezuela." The Army Transport Command was to provide the shipping to transport the JLAs to America.[13] The lack of shipping space, the intransigence and international bungling of working through third countries (Spain and Switzerland), and the impending defeat of Japan, made further exchanges impossible.

By 1943, of those repatriated to Japan, 36.1% were from Peru. Many at Crystal City demanded that they be returned to Peru since their homes and properties were there—yet Peru was adamant in refusing to allow them to return.[14] Later, after the war, those with Peruvian citizenship had some success returning to their native country.

At War's End

By 1944 the INS had 1,400 Japanese Peruvians on hand and by V-J Day there were 1,333 left in the U.S.[15] The intransigence of Peru in accepting its former residents posed anew a distinct problem for the U.S. State Department. State Department personnel were unsure that the U.S. had legal authority to repatriate Japanese from Latin America. They were brought forcibly during the war to the U.S. The State Department could eject all aliens brought here if they proved to be a threat to the security of the United States. The Japanese Latin Americans, the greatest majority being Peruvians, were peaceful, quiescent and law abiding.

With subtle pressures advanced by the INS, such as circulating reports of the impending closure of all camps, and the Peruvian government's refusal to accept them, the remaining Japanese Peruvians, singly and group-wise, were faced with a gut wrenching decision. Should they return to a devastated Japan—a Japan that they had left years ago, a Japan that their children had never seen nor were citizens of? The INS and State Department assured free passage to Japan. But many of the Japanese, especially those with propertied holdings in Peru, insisted that they as Peruvians must be allowed to return to Peru. A few, less than 300, more in bewilderment rather than taking calculated risks, hoped that they would be permitted to somehow, some way, be allowed to remain in the U.S.

Of importance is the fact that our State Department took another strange tact in disavowing the illegal and inhumane methods resorted to in shipping Japanese Latin Americans to the U.S. *Now it blamed the Peruvian government entirely for Japanese Peruvian "illegal" entry into the U.S.* The State Department was anxious to step out of the human drama which affected thousands of unfortunate Japanese. Peru, for its part, turned a deaf ear to all of their own citizens and long time residents of Japanese ancestry who were imploring them to allow their return. At the same time, the Peruvian government willingly accepted their deported German and Italian residents from the U.S. camps.[16]

In early 1946 the Peruvian government muddied the diplomatic negotiations between the U.S. and Peru when it began accepting selectively some Japanese to include non-Peruvian Japanese. The U.S. State Department pondered this action and hinted at the probabilities of bribery, favoritism and irregular procedures by certain high Peruvian government officials.[17]   In turn, the State Department declared the Japanese Latin Americans as "alien enemies," basing its decision on a   Federal Court of Southern District of New York ruling (January 10, 1946).   According to the court, as enemy aliens, Japanese Peruvians could be deported under the Alien Enemy Act of 1798, and the State Department hurried to hold hearings on the Japanese internees.

Repatriation To Japan

Bewildered, disheartened, without hope, feeling betrayed and pressured by the U.S. government, hundreds of Japanese Peruvians signed on to return to Japan.[18] Dissention ensued in the camps as pro Japan supporters decried the pro-Peru and pro-U.S.A. groups with bitterness: "How can you, a member of the Yamato race, turn your back on the homeland?" "How can you possibly return to a country who callously deported you—you who always obeyed Peru's laws?" "How can you forgive the Americans for putting you within barbed wire enclosures where armed guards occupy watch towers?"   In defense of their decision those remaining retorted, "I do not wish to go to Japan—I have never been to Japan—I was born in Peru and I feel that Peru is my country." Another declared, "My children were born in the United States. I wish to stay in the United States with the whole family and I wish to educate my children in the United States."[19]

The Fight To Become U.S. Residents

The saga of Japanese Peruvians to stay in the U.S. is long and tortuous. Sixty eight families elected not to return to Japan or Peru.

This posed a distinct problem for the INS and State Department as all of these families had petitioned the State Department for permanent residency. The problem was that the INS, through State Department directives, had declared them "Illegal immigrants" and had confiscated their passports even as they were summarily dumped on our shores through our wartime action based on Peruvian and American racism and war hysteria.

The INS even issued warrants for their arrest as "illegals." Desperate, the families wrote imploring letters and appeals to President Truman, Secretary of State Byrnes, Attorney General Clark and even Catholic church authorities, to quash the impending deportation to Japan. It almost appeared as though they were grasping at straws as time became a crucial factor.

It is at this point that two attorneys, A. L. Wirin and Wayne M. Collins, entered the cause for Japanese Peruvian justice. Both were experienced civil liberties attorneys, and both had fought for individual freedoms under the banner of the American Civil Liberties Union.

Collins, in particular, had fought hard for the Japanese Americans.[20] With his signal victory in the Mitsuye Endo case, which restored to her all civil liberties and the right to leave camp and return to her home in California, and with the subsequent revocation of the banning of Japanese Americans from the West Coast, the spirit of the remaining Japanese Peruvians took on a hopeful measure.

Filing stays of deportation in the Federal District Court of Northern California, Wirin, Collins, and Ernest Besig (also of the ACLU) were able to defeat attempts of the INS to deport the Japanese Peruvians to Japan. Some (about 110) who had sponsors and had been released from INS custody, were permitted to join their sponsors in various parts of the United States. A few of those detained by warrants were permitted by Peru to return.

As the Crystal City internees bade farewell to the year 1945, uncertainty still prevailed concerning their final status. In 1946 the Peruvian government made it clear that it would allow three categories of Japanese Peruvians to return: (1) those born in Peru (Nisei);

(2) naturalized citizens; and (3) those married to Peruvians. Based on this new declaration, over 100 were able to return to Peru in 1946.

The Seabrook Farms Story

Seabrook Farms, in New Jersey, was a large corporate truck farming and food freezing establishment. By 1943 they were in dire need of farm labor and decided to employ young adult Japanese Americans to work at Seabrook Farms. By December, 1945, 1,024 Japanese American men and women proved to be their most diligent, efficient workers.

Attorney Collins saw the Seabrook Farms situation as an alternative for those waiting final determination of their status by the State Department and INS. With their own Japanese American workers returning to their homes or continuing their education, Seabrook Farms decided to recruit the Japanese Peruvians still left at Crystal City. Over 200 Japanese Peruvians were recruited to work, and they proved to be just as hard-working and reliable as the Japanese Americans. Hours were long, some days lasting twelve hours, and many worked seven days a week. Wages were from 52.5 cents an hour on the production line (mostly females) to 62.5 cents in the field or on the docks where hard labor was required. Later the wages were increased to 55.5 cents and 67.5 cents.[21]

The impact on the Japanese Peruvians as they left behind the barbed wire fence enclosures and constant INS dictum of camp life was devastating. They had not grappled with the everyday realities of living in a free, open economy. Food, clothing, education of their children in American schools, transportation into the surrounding towns, housing, medical concerns, all became profound problems for the Japanese Peruvians. During incarceration they had not had to grapple with these mundane day-to-day problems. Now these became almost life and death issues.

Insensitive bureaucratic practices, both by Peru and the U.S.A, held the Japanese Peruvians on a mad, roller coaster ride concerning their desire to stay in the United States. Those left at

Seabrook held on to a hope, faint though it might be. They felt the longer their stay in Seabrook, the better the chances that they would be allowed to become residents of America.

By early 1947, of the 2,000 plus Japanese Latin Americans, over 90% being Japanese Peruvians, all brought unwillingly into the U.S., only 298 Japanese Peruvians were left: 178 at Seabrook Farm, 96 at Crystal City, 26 paroled elsewhere in the US, and three who were hospitalized. As they agonized through the weeks and months, with petitions and letters of support being sent in by the papal nuncio, and Cardinal Guevara, Archbishop of Lima, the National Catholic Welfare Conference in Washington, and the Japanese American Citizens League, they held on to their hopes.[22] The long practiced Japanese cultural norm of "*gambare*," (never give up) shone through and continued to buoy their spirits.

Attorney Collins worked ceaselessly for their cause, sending letters, appeals, and petitions to the President of Peru, U.S. Secretary of State George Marshall and influential members of the U.S. Congress—all reminding them of the inhumanities that both governments had visited upon the Japanese Peruvians.

Success—But Limited Relief For
The Japanese Peruvians

The long and harried road to win their right to stay in America finally came to an end in late 1947, albeit from an unexpected source. Guatemalan German internee Max Paetau had appealed his deportation order and the U.S. Circuit of Appeals ruled in his favor stating: "An alien seized by the United States elsewhere, and brought to the United States against his will for internment for security reasons as an alien enemy cannot be deported as an 'immigrant,' at least not before he has been afforded an opportunity to depart voluntarily."

Yet, the wheels of national and international bureaucracy turned all too slowly. For those desiring to return to Peru, the Peruvian government threw up roadblocks, delayed, and continued to urge the U.S. to hold on to the Japanese Peruvians. They would accept a distinct minimum, and then only if they were Peruvian nationals, or married to Peruvians. Consequently, less than five percent of those taken from Peru were ever able to return. The greatest majority of the 2,000 plus Japanese Latin Americans interned in the U.S. were deported to Japan.

Despite the U.S. State Department's memorandum issued in 1949, which stated that "the obvious solution is to regularize their status in the United States as permanent immigrants legally admitted," it would be thirteen years, to 1955, before the final case for permanent residence was settled. At long last every Japanese Peruvian who had been uprooted had found a home, in Japan, Peru, or the United States.[23]

On 31 August, 1954, Public Law 751 was amended to read: "Any alien who establishes that prior to July 31, 1953 he . . . was brought to the United States from other American republics for internment, may, not later than June 30, 1955, apply to the Attorney General of the United States for an adjustment of his immigration status."[24]

Those who had chosen and persevered to remain in the U.S. were finally free from the grasping clutches of the INS. Many went to Chicago for job opportunities and others proceeded to the west coast to join their Peruvian and American Nisei brethren. Their tortuous travails and legal problems having ended, the 298 Peruvian Japanese finally began their road to become Japanese Americans.

Epilogue

The vicissitudes of Japanese Peruvians continue. When the Civil Liberties Act of 1988 was signed into law by President Reagan the law included only those who were permanent residents or citizens of the U.S. during war time. The law did not include illegal aliens and that meant that Japanese Latin Americans who were imprisoned in the U.S. camps are not eligible to receive any funds, nor an apology from the U.S. government.

Attempts have been made to include Japanese Latin

Americans in awarding them compensation based on the Civil Liberties Act of 1988 but all have failed, and the provisions of the Act expired in 1998. The Japanese American Citizens League, and other ethnic civil rights organizations, are now supporting further attempts among redress activists to provide compensation and a congressional apology to those interned Japanese Latin Americans of World War II.[25] That political ploy, at this juncture, given congress' anti-immigration mood, a Herculean task at best, may prove unsuccessful.

This essay is intended to relate and publicize the ignominious, international wrong doing on the part of two governments, the United States and Peru. Our government surreptitiously aided and abetted the Peruvian government who quietly kidnapped and forced certain Japanese Peruvians and their families to be shipped to America to be imprisoned in the INS camps. Their civil and human rights were totally disregarded. Some were even tortured by the Peruvian police. Truly, this ignoble action, perpetrated by the two governments in the so-called exigencies of war, should be further publicized and appropriate redress compensation be awarded. Alien rights are as precious as citizen rights and all governments need to take special heed to provide aliens protection, security, justice and well being even during war time.

Notes

1. Camp Kenedy, Texas, Crystal City, Texas, etc.

2. Niigata, Okayama, Hiroshima, Yamaguchi, Fukuoka, Kumamoto and Okinawa prefectures. Drought had stricken the Inland Sea Area in the 1880s.

3. Gardiner, pp. 5-6.

4. Gardiner, pp. 7-8.

5. Emmerson, p.130.

6. Over 3,000 civilians were captured in China and more than 5,000

were captured in the Philippines.

7. Undersecretary of State Sumner Welles and Attorney General Francis Biddle agreed that such internees would be under the jurisdiction of the Immigration and Naturalization Service—they had no comprehension of the enormity of the problem.

8. Gardiner, p.21.

9. Kunio Takeshita was picked up at his house in Lima. Arturo Shinei Yakabi was an unfortunate bakery employee who was a sacrificial lamb. His employer had paid off the police and took Yakabi in his place. Yakabi could have been released if he'd had money to bribe the police, (Gardiner, pp. 72-73).

10. Hosokawa, pp. 8-9.

11. Crystal City is located 120 miles southwest of San Antonio and the camp was a one-time migratory farm laborers' camp. It consisted of 41 small three-room cottages, 118 one-room buildings and some utilities structures. INS also built 219 temporary housing units of duplex, triplex and quadruplex design, 15 additional three-room cottages, and 103 plywood huts . It accommodated 962 families, mostly Japanese, with a few German families (Gardiner, pp. 56-61).

12. Crystal City alumni hold large reunions every three to five years and returnees come back from all over the world. See *Crystal City Reunion Book*, 1993.

13. Gardiner, p.13.

14. Peru's ambassador to the U.S., Pedro Beltrain, wanted all Japanese out of Peru and demanded that the U.S. accept all Japanese-Peruvians and deport them to Japan (Gardiner, p.108).

15. Gardiner, p.112.

16. Gardiner, p.132.

17. Gardiner, p.133.

18. 660 Japanese Peruvians left from Crystal City on the *SS Matsonia* in early December, 1946. 135 left for Japan on the *General*

Randall on 25 November, 1946, and 17 Japanese Peruvians joined 4,241 Japanese Americans sailing for Japan on the *General Gordon*, sailing on 29 December, l946. By 1947 all who chose to return to Japan had been deported.

19. At the time of this statement (1946-7) chances for the Japanese Peruvians wanting to stay in America were very slim at best.

20. Collins had argued and lost in the Korematsu case where he attacked the constitutionality of the Japanese-American evacuation. But in the Mitsuye Endo case, where Collins had her petition for a writ of *habeus corpus* demanding that her liberty be restored and that she should not be held against her will and be confined in the camps, he won. This was the tact that Collins subsequently pursued—that Japanese-Peruvians were being held against their will.

21. Gardiner, p. 158.

22. Gardiner, p. 157.

23. Gardiner, p. 171.

24. Shimizu, pp. 9-10.

25. In Carmen Mochizuki vs. United States, Federal Judge Loren A. Smith decreed that "all of the surviving former Japanese-Latin-American WWII internees and their immediate families receive a presidential letter of apology. Only about a half of the 676 JLA petitioners will receive $5,000 redress payments, since the $1.6 billion fund set up in the 1988 Civil Liberties Act has but $2.82 million remaining in the Civil Liberties Fund (Pacific Citizen, #2860/Vol. 128, No. 2, 22 Jan - 4 Feb., 1999, p.1).

Bibliography

Barnhart, Edward, "Japanese Internees From Peru," in *Pacific Historical Review*, 31, No. 2, May 1962.

Collaer, N.D. "The Crystal City Internment Camp", *INS Monthly Review*, 5, No. 6, December, 1947, pp. 75-77.

Conn, Stetson. "Authorizing The Secretary of War To Prescribe

Military Areas" Executive Order 9066 (http://www.library.arizona.edu/images/jpamer/execordr.html, 1/16/97).*Crystal City Internment Camp 50th Anniversary Reunion Album*, (Monterey, CA: 8-10 October, 1993).

Dower, John W., *War Without Mercy: Race And Power In The Pacific War* (New York, NY: Pantheon Books, 1986).

Drinnon, Richard *Keeper Of Concentration Camps: Dillon S. Meyer And American Racism*, (Berkeley, CA: University of California Press, 1987).

Emmerson, John. *The Japanese Thread*, (Winston, NY:, 1978).

Gardiner, C. Harvey, *Pawns In A Triangle Of Hate: The Peruvian Japanese And The United States*, (Seattle, WA: 1981).

_____, *The Japanese And Peru, 1873-1973* (Albuquerque, NM: University of New Mexico Press, 1975).

Higashide, Seiichi, *Adios To Tears* (Honolulu, HI: E & E Kudo, 1993).

Honda, Harry K. "Three Nisei Deported From Peru In WWII Sue U.S. For Redress," *Pacific Citizen* (Monterey Park, CA: 20 Sep. - 3 Oct, 1996, p.1).

_____, "ABC Unlike Peru," *Pacific Citizen*, 4-17 Oct., 1996, p.10.

Hosokawa, Bill, "Mr. Estrada, Listen to Emmerson, not Baker," *Pacific Citizen*, 21 March - 3 April 1997, pp. 8-9.

INS File #2213, RG 60, Washington National Records Center, Suitland, MD.

Irons, Peter, *Justice At War: The Story Of The Japanese American Internment Cases* (New York, NY: Oxford University Press, 1983).

_____, ed., *Justice Delayed: The Record Of The Japanese Internet Cases* (Middletown, CT: Wesleyan University Press, 1989).

Kaneshiro, Takeo, *Internees: War Relocation Center Memoirs And Diaries*: (New York, NY: Vantage Press, 1976).

Marutani, Bill, "Doing The Right Thing," *Pacific Citizen*, 4-17 Oct., 1996, p.10.

Myers, Roger, "War Relocation Authority Camps in Arizona, 1942-1946," University of Arizona Library's Special Collection, http://www.library.arizpma.edu/images/jpamer/wrintro.html (1/16/97 4:51)

Nakatsu, Russ, "Historical Background on the Kibei: Caught Between Cultures—The Kibei," rnakatsu@kent.wednet.edu., (04/12/96).

Personal Justice Denied : *Report of the Commission on Wartime Relocation and Internment of Civilians* (Washington, DC: Government Printing Office, 1982).

Rucker, Warren Page, *The U.S.-Peruvian Policy Towards Peruvian Japanese During World War II* (M.A. Thesis, University of Virginia, 1970).

Sawada, Mitzko, "After The Camps: Seabrook Farms, New Jersey and the Resettlement of Japanese Americans, 1944-47," *Amerasia Journal*, vol. 13.2, 1986-87, pp. 117-136.

Shimizu, Grace, "Japanese Peruvians," National Japanese American Historical Society, *Nikkei Heritage*, vol. 8, No. 2, Spring, 1996.

Steinberg, Alfred, "Blunder Maroons Peruvian Japanese in the U.S.," *Washington Post*, Section 2, 26 September, 1942, pp. 1, 4.

Tateishi, John, *And Justice For All: An Oral History Of The Japanese: American Detention Camps* (New York, NY: Random House, 1984).

Thomas, Dorothy S., *The Salvage* (Berkeley, CA: University of California Press, 1969).

Thomas, Dorothy S. and Richard Nishimoto, *The Spoilage* (Berkeley, CA: University of California Press, 1969).

Tigner, James L., *The Orientals In Los Angeles* (Ph.D. Dissertation, Stanford University, 1956).

126

"Timeline," http://www.geocities.com/Athens/8420/timeline.html (1/1697)

Weglyn, Michi, *Years Of Infamy: The Untold Story Of Americas Concentration Camps* (New York, NY: William Morrow and Co., 1976).

CHAPTER EIGHT

"TOKYO ROSE"—THE VICTIM OF A LEGEND

Introduction

Japanese-Americans have contributed mightily to the war efforts of their country. We have seen this to be so in the recounting of the exploits of the 100th infantry Battalion and the 442nd Regimental Combat Team. The one case which might cast doubt on the loyalty and commitment of Japanese Americans to their country is that of "Tokyo Rose," the person who was accused of cooperating with the Japanese and thus branded a traitor to her country. Because it was such a famous case, it has, perhaps, cast aspersions upon Japanese Americans far beyond its real significance. For that reason alone it is worth revisiting. The purpose of this chapter is to illustrate and prove that Iva Ikuko Toguri d'Aquino, the woman known as "Tokyo Rose," was truly a victim of racism—racism that made her a tragic victim of a wartime legend.

Iva Toguri's Story

Iva Toguri was born on July 4, 1916, in Los Angeles, California. The Toguri family lived in a predominantly white neighborhood, were members of the Methodist Church, and most of her friends were Caucasians. So Iva had little knowledge of the Japanese language and culture. Like many young, aspiring Niseis[1] of that period, she concentrated on her studies, became a skilled typist[2] and pianist and graduated from UCLA in June, 1941.

Shortly after graduation Iva's family learned that her maternal aunt, in Tokyo, was seriously ill and on the verge of death. Iva's mother was precariously ill, too, and so Iva was selected to go to Japan to help nurse her aunt. She was in Tokyo by 24 July, 1941. As U.S.-Japanese relations worsened, Iva's father urged her to come home on the next vessel sailing to America, the *S.S. Tatsuta Maru,* which was to leave Yokohama, Japan, on December first. Iva was unable to book passage, but no matter. The ship was recalled as the Pearl Harbor attack occurred while the vessel was on the high seas.

At the time, Iva was living with her uncle and aunt, Hajime Hattori. Within a matter of days after Pearl Harbor, the *Kempeitai,* the Japanese Army's Thought Control Police, visited Iva and demanded that she renounce her U.S. citizenship and apply for Japanese citizenship. She flatly refused and with that they classified her as an undesirable enemy alien. She was denied food rations, her movements were restricted and she was constantly harassed by the Thought Police. The harassment from the Police and the neighbors became so intense for all the Hattoris that her uncle and aunt asked her to live somewhere else. From that moment she was on her own—without a food ration card and without a job. She faced starvation. She even asked the authorities to imprison her so she would not be without food or lodging but they refused. By June, 1943, due to a limited diet caused by her lack of funds, Iva suffered from malnutrition and beriberi. Finally she found a part time job at the *Domei* News Agency as a typist. In August, 1943, she took on a second part time job as a typist at Radio Tokyo (*NHK—Nippon Hoso Kaisha*) .[3]

During the same month Iva met three POWs who were working as broadcasters at Radio Tokyo: Major Charles H. Cousens, an Australian, Captain Wallace E. Ince, an American, and Lieutenant Norman Reyes, a Filipino. All three had been severely threatened, abused and bulldozed into writing and making propaganda broadcasts for the Japanese Imperial Army by Overseas Bureau Chief Major Shigetsugu Tsuneishi.[4] Iva was very sympathetic to the three men for they represented a thread of connection to her American heritage, and she occasionally shared some of her contraband food and medicine (aspirin, yeast pills, and quinine) with them. The POWs' broadcasts went well once they began to write all the materials themselves and especially when Lt. Reyes began introducing the "Zero Hour" programs with American big band music. In fact the program came to be entertainment looked forward to by American personnel in Guadalcanal. As they reported: "Tokyo has been beaming a program called the 'Zero Hour' direct to the Russell Islands and Guadalcanal. The fellows like it very much because it cries over them and feels so sorry for them. It talks about the food that they miss by not being home and tells how the war workers are stealing their jobs and girls."[5]

Major Tsuneishi was elated with the seemingly smooth delivery of the propaganda programs of the POWs when contrasted with the boring, halting, ineffective broadcasts presented by his Japanese announcers. He decided to expand the programs from 15 minutes to 30 to 45 minutes. Cousens read edited POW messages, Ince broadcast local U.S.A. disaster happenings, while Reyes played favorite tunes like a disc jockey. Since the three wrote the script, they were able to control the nature of the program and they had cleverly used slang, double *entendres*, and read demoralizing news items hurriedly, or in a joking tone of voice. In essence, the announcers were subverting the nature of the programs and they became entertainment to the American GIs.[6] Reacting to Tsuneishi's demand for longer "Zero Hour" programming and hopeful in continuing to control the nature of the program, Cousens decided to recruit friendly typist Iva Toguri to becoming an announcer. At first Toguri declined saying that "I was hired to work as a typist, not as an announcer. I have no experience as an announcer, I don't know the first thing about announcing.[7]

Ince and Reyes also questioned Cousens' choice saying "she's got a voice like a crow—deep and cracked. Another even said "she's got a voice like a farmer." But Cousens would not be swayed and said "My plan in using her is to make a complete burlesque of our program. She has a gin fog voice, rough—almost masculine, anything but a feminine voice."[8] Daily, Cousens coached reluctant Iva Toguri to speak slowly, cheerfully and when Iva complained about being selected by the POWs to her supervisor, Shigechika Takano, he replied, "You are a foreigner—you have no choice, the Army has ordered you to broadcast. I don't think there's any need to tell you what will happen if you don't do it."[9]

There were other women broadcasters there at NHK with smooth, mellifluous voices, but Cousens wanted Iva's distinctive, harsh, throaty voice and he coached her pattern to be like Gracie Allen's—comical, cheerful, lively and gay.[10] Her voice was an immediate hit with the GIs. To the GIs Iva's voice was comical, certainly not the exotic, sexy, mysterious, seductive and pliant oriental female usually conjured in the minds of lonely western servicemen. This was Cousen's subterfuge—he wanted the GIs to guffaw and laugh at the program rather than be propagandized. Cousens wanted her to use a *nom de plume* and suggested "Orphan Ann of the Pacific." (Ann being an abbreviation from "announcer," and Pacific GIs were often referred in the news as orphans in the Pacific theater.)[11]

"Tokyo Rose" was never used by Iva or any of the other female announcers. It was very probably a term concocted by American GIs who had at times referred to the voice as "Radio Rose" and hence to "Tokyo Rose" since Tokyo was assumed by all to be the broadcasting center for Japan. In fact, the U.S. Office of War Information investigated the phenomenon and said:

> There is no Tokyo Rose; the name is strictly a GI invention. The name has been applied to at least two lilting Japanese voices on the Japanese radio. . . . Government monitors listening in twenty four hours a day have never heard the words Tokyo Rose over a Japanese controlled Far Eastern radio.[12]

Unfortunately, Cousens collapsed from a heart attack in June 1944 and Iva was lost without his script writing, his coaching, his encouragements—they were a team in the attempt to sabotage the propaganda broadcasts. The "Zero Hour" programs lost their vitality with the loss of Cousens' script-writing and as air raids increased Iva found numerous excuses to skip work. Thereupon other Nisei

women pitched in and did the broadcasts.[13] This caused a rift
between Iva and the other women at the American section of NHK.
Iva had better pay and more privileges since Major Tsuneishi felt that
Iva was the best announcer for the "Zero Hour" program.

It was during this period (19 April, 1945, the day after she
converted to Roman Catholicism) that Felipe D'Aquino married Iva
and he urged her to quit. Iva had a second good paying job at the
Danish Legation and they felt that she did not have to face the antagonism of the jealous American section's women staff members. But
Major Tsuneishi would not release her—he wanted "Orphan Ann" on
his propaganda program.

By April, 1945 it was clear that Japan would lose and as the
air raids became more frequent Iva refused to come in to Tokyo from
her home in Atsugi to do the broadcasts. In fact, two others, Miyeko
Furuya, and Mary Ishii, did the "Zero Hour" segment of the propaganda broadcasts.[14]

And suddenly with the atom bombing of Hiroshima and
Nagasaki the war was over. Felipe and Iva were overjoyed. She had
fought her best against the propaganda authorities of Tokyo and even
aided the Allied POWs—she was victorious. She believed in
America and where others tried to convince her to renounce her
American citizenship she refused to do so. Yet, legends are almost
impossible to squelch and so began the travails of Iva Toguri
D'Aquino.

With the end of the war correspondents poured into Tokyo
and almost all wanted to interview Tokyo Rose. The first two to
reach Iva were Clark Lee (International News Service) and Harry
Brundidge(*Cosmopolitan* Magazine) and she was promised $2,000
by the magazine if she agreed to an exclusive interview—this was 1
September, 1945.[15] Competing correspondents were also interviewing other Nisei women who were involved in the "Zero Hour" broadcasts but Iva gradually outdistanced the others in publicity. In fact,
she naïvely signed the contract as "Iva Ikuko Toguri" (Tokyo Rose).

Unfortunately, she never received the $2,000. After the interview done by Clark Lee, the *Los Angeles Examiner* front page headlines of 3 September read: "TRAITOR'S PAY. . . . The one and only Tokyo Rose, a Los Angeles born American of Japanese ancestry...."[16] Thus, Iva, by her naïveté and willingness to please seemingly trustworthy fellow Americans, plus the desire to be rid of other correspondents as well as to be paid the large sum of $2,000, did not then realize the enormity of the stakes at hand—so she then signed the seventeen page interview at Lee's urging: "To Clark Lee, who interviewed me at the Imperial Hotel on September 1. Iva Toguri 'Tokyo Rose.'"[17]

Lee's damaging "scoop" caused the anti-Japanese elements of southern California to scream loudly that Iva Toguri was a traitor. Politically ambitious Charles H. Carr, United States attorney for the region of Southern California, declared: "This infamous woman—born here and educated here—used myriad artifices and devices to spread discontent and dissension among American troops. This should be a matter for local court action rather than court martial proceedings."[18]

The anti-Japanese sentiment in California and the United States at this time can be seen by the following:[19]

- More violence was committed against Japanese Americans returning to California than during the post Pearl Harbor days.

- The August 1946 National Opinion Research poll showed that two thirds of all Americans believed that Japanese Americans spied for Japan.

- Only 13% of Americans believed that Japanese Americans had no part in espionage activities against America.

- Immigration from Japan was still banned.

- 4,724 persons of Japanese ancestry were deported after

the war—nearly 50% of them were children of the parents deported.

- Asian women were still caricatured as seductive temptresses in comic strips such as "Terry and the Pirates," and "Steve Canyon."

Arrest of Iva Toguri as Tokyo Rose

On 17 October, 1945, Iva was summarily arrested and hauled in by the CIC (Counter Intelligence Corps) in Yokohama and held incommunicado at Sugamo Prison. Her husband Felipe could only visit her for twenty minutes once a month. After intensive grilling by Army CIC and the FBI, she was cleared and released on 25 October, 1946, fully a year later. The U.S. Justice Department had concluded that there was insufficient evidence to bring charges against her. It appeared that Iva and Felipe could now begin life anew in Tokyo, but that was not to be.

In 1947 Iva became pregnant, with the baby due in January, 1948. She desperately wanted her child to be born in America to lay claim to her cherished American citizenship. She wanted to go home. She had already learned that her mother had died in 1942 in the Tulare Assembly Center and that her father and brother had relocated to Chicago. But the FBI, Harry Brundidge, and radio columnist Walter Winchell, pounded away in yellow journalistic style that she was the traitorous Tokyo Rose. Soon, without any new evidence that would assure conviction, they urged Attorney General Tom C. Clark, through the Immigration and Naturalization Service, to deny her application to return. The unknowing American public was further swayed by protests and resolutions against her return issued by the American Legion, Native Sons and Daughters of the Golden West, and the Los Angeles City Council.[20]

Brundidge even resurrected Clark Lee's old notes and claimed that they were Iva's confessions that she was Tokyo Rose. When Attorney General Clark rejected the notes as improper evidence Brundidge, with aid from FBI Director J. Edgar Hoover, convinced the government to provide him free air transportation to Tokyo where he would obtain Iva's signature indicating that Lee's notes concerning her Tokyo Rose activities and appellations were accurate. Accompanying Brundidge to Tokyo was John Hogan, a Justice Department lawyer. When Brundidge met Iva in Tokyo she reread the notes and flatly denied the accuracy. At this juncture Brundidge, realizing Iva's great desire to return home, cleverly persuaded Iva to sign the notes, saying, "If you sign these notes you will be assured of going home."

Iva was tired and she desperately wanted to return to America so she naïvely signed. She had no counsel to advise her. In fact, Hogan did not even advise her of her rights and glibly remarked to her, "You'll probably be indicted for treason but they'll never hang a woman and you'll probably get a short sentence. Anyway, you'll get back to the United States."[21]

Having signed the notes, Iva Toguri was rearrested on 26 August, 1948 and charged with treason. In overseas treason cases, according to U.S. law, the trial must take place wherever the accused first returns to American soil. Attorney General Clark proclaimed that she would not be accorded a fair trial in California and implied that Hawaii would be too sympathetic to her cause, so plans were drawn to have her flown over Mexico or Canada and brought to the east coast. Clark, however, was persuaded to change his mind and so he ordered the trial to be held in San Francisco, a city with a strong anti-Japanese legacy.

The Tokyo Rose Trial

Iva's father, Jun Toguri, and sister June, met Iva in the U.S. Marshal's office in San Francisco for a very brief period. Though Iva was without a passport and clearly not dangerous, she was refused bail and was imprisoned at Fort Mason. Her father said, "Girl, I'm proud of you—You didn't give up your U.S. citizenship!" The Toguris searched long and hard for an attorney to defend her but

Iva Toguri in Tokyo, 1948. (U.S. Army Signal Corps photo, courtesy Library of Congress).

unlike the protest years of the 60's and 70's, prominent and effective defense attorneys passed on her case. Also, the Toguris were poor and the case would not enhance the lawyer's careers. Finally, a liberal, 49 year old attorney, very experienced in civil rights cases, stepped forth and agreed to defend Iva for court and legal costs only, no lawyer's fees. He was Wayne M. Collins, well known for his defense of Nisei Fred Korematsu who challenged the government's order to move all Japanese Americans from the west coast. Now she was in the hands of an able, experienced lawyer who advised her of her individual rights immediately. The FBI could not grill her without Collins at her side. At this stage, Iva had already spent almost two years in prison, including the time that she was imprisoned in Japan

.   Iva was charged with eight counts of treason.[22] According to the Constitution: "Treason against the United States shall consist only in levying war against them, or adhering to their enemies, giving them aid and comfort. No person shall be convicted of treason unless on the testimony of two witnesses to the same overt act."[23]

Judge Michael Roche allowed the prosecution to subpoena nineteen Japanese witnesses from Occupied Japan, but none were allowed the defense. Despite having eight nonwhites (six African Americans and two Asian Americans) on the first jury list, all were removed by peremptory challenges. Eventually an all white jury of six white males and six white females were seated.

Clark Lee could only testify concerning the interview, and Harry Brundidge was accused of bribing a Japanese coworker to falsely claim that he saw and heard Iva Toguri make anti-American broadcasts, so he was not called by the prosecution to testify. Several U.S. veterans were called to testify but each contradicted each other on the voice, accent, theme song, time of program, etc.—all the result of them hearing different women, different programs, at different times, and from different locations, truly a strong indication that there was no one person doing propaganda broadcasts from Tokyo and that Tokyo Rose was but a myth, a legend, built up in the minds of lonely American romanticist servicemen.

The prosecution's trial depended on witnesses subpoenaed from Occupied Japan. Former Lieutenant Colonel Shigetsugu Tsuneishi, Chief of Propaganda Broadcasting, testified that several female announcers were employed for the "Zero Hour" program and that they had broadcast from thirteen different stations other than Tokyo.

Ironically, the critical witnesses to testify against Iva were two Nisei men born in America: George Mitsushio, the civilian chief of the "Zero Hour" program and Kenkichi Oki, production supervisor at Radio Tokyo.[24] Both men claimed Japanese citizenship under the *Jus Sanguinis* laws of Japan by registering themselves in the *Koseki Tohon* (Family Registry). However, both men had not renounced their American citizenship to the U.S. Consul and so, legally, they were dual citizens and could have been charged as traitors by the American government. Oki testified that they had been sent under duress by the Occupation authorities and, later, both men admitted that they had been forced to lie. Iva Toguri was forced to trial for treason because she steadfastly held on to her American citizenship while her two accusers were in reality "turncoats" against America.

Charles Cousens, who flew in voluntarily from Australia, and Wallace Ince and Norman Reyes all testified in her defense that Iva was a loyal American who did not make traitorous broadcasts, that she played light, entertaining music for the servicemen and often aided them by bringing food and medicines despite warnings by the Japanese officers not to aid the POWs. Iva, in her own defense, testified that she did not betray America. She believed that she was playing light music for entertainment. She did not renounce her U.S. citizenship and always remained loyal to America despite threats and penalties.

The trial lasted 56 days and cost the government $500,000, the most expensive up to that period. In an early ballot the jury was deadlocked at ten to 2 for acquittal on all counts. After another 20 hours the jury informed Judge Roche that they were still deadlocked, but the Judge would not rule for a hung jury and urged them to do "their patriotic duty." Newspaper writers and court spectators were clearly in favor of the defendant. The writers had even indicated the strong bias of Judge Roche against the defendant. Finally, after three days, on 29 September, 1949, the jury announced their verdict: Innocent on seven counts, guilty on one count. Iva was declared guilty for one "overt act." The act: "On a day during October, 1944, the exact date being to the Grand Jurors unknown, the defendant, in the offices of the Broadcasting Corporation of Japan, did speak into a microphone concerning the loss of ships."[25]

Iva was adjudged guilty for reading over the air shortly after the Battle of Leyte Gulf: "Orphans of the Pacific, you really are orphans now. How will you get home now that all your ships are sunk.?" Amazing! This despite everyone knowing that the Leyte Gulf battle was a stunning, overwhelming victory for the U.S. Clearly the jurors were fatigued, grasping for straws, and wanting to end the long trial to go home.

On 7 October, 1949, Judge Roche sentenced Iva Toguri to ten years of imprisonment, plus a $10,000 fine. Iva automatically lost her treasured American citizenship because of her conviction of treason.

In addition, her husband Felipe d'Aquino was forced to sign a statement that he would never try to reenter the United States and was taken back to Occupied Japan.[26] Iva was imprisoned at Alderson Federal Reformatory for Women in West Virginia, and after serving for six years and two months, reduced time gained for good behavior, she was released on 28 January, 1956. Appeals had been filed all the way to the Supreme Court but they were all denied. She went to Chicago to live with her father, brother and sister.

If Iva thought her nightmare was over, she was sadly mistaken. Because the news media considered her "hot property," a headline screamed: "TOKYO ROSE QUITS JAIL SHOWS NO REPENTANCE."[27]

The INS Harassment of Iva Toguri

As soon as she was released the Immigration and Naturalization Service began deportation action claiming that Iva was an "undesirable alien" and subject to deportation under terms of the Walter-McCarran Act of 1952. The discriminatory facet of the action was that the Act was *ex post facto* , and exile was not a part of her sentence; yet, the government gave her thirty days to leave the country or be deported. The INS restricted her travel to no more than fifty miles from Chicago. They had cruelly kept her in their clutches. It was not until 1958 that her attorney, Wayne Collins, was able to have the deportation order quashed.

In 1968, the persecution of Iva Toguri continued as the Justice Department ordered her to pay the $10,000 in full. She was poverty stricken and unable to pay so the government seized her life insurance policy worth $4,745 and later collected the balance from the assets willed to her by her father. Thus ended the government's collective harassment of Iva Toguri.[28]

Restoration of American Citizenship
and the Pardon

During her long period of investigation, trial, and incarceration, Iva Toguri was without any organizational support whatsoever. The Niseis themselves were hard at work trying to reestablish themselves in their schooling, jobs and communities—and they did not want to jeopardize their acceptance into the majority by championing the cause of another Nisei accused of treason. Liberal civil rights type organizations were afraid of McCarthyism and did not risk possible charges by defending Iva.

In time, however, the upward socioeconomic mobility and the general social acceptance of the Nisei, the developments in Vietnam and of Watergate, may have influenced the Niseis to conclude that the U.S. government had horribly mistreated Iva Toguri. Dr. Clifford Uyeda, a former president of the Japanese American Citizen's League, garnered the strong support of the JACL, and he formed the National Committee for Iva Toguri in San Francisco on April 2, 1975. The committee concluded that their national organization must come to the aid of Iva and help restore her American citizenship. "How?" was the obvious query—the courts, all the way to the Supreme Court, had previously denied her appeals.

The only avenue of hope was a presidential pardon. Dr. Uyeda with the wise counsel of Federal District Court Judge Robert Takasugi of Los Angeles, led the seemingly impossible task of mobilizing public support for Iva. The public, to include Niseis, they said, must be "reeducated" and speak out against the discriminatory treatment accorded Iva, and destroy for all time the legend of Tokyo Rose—a legend that dogged and devastated Iva's life.

Iva wanted desperately to be pardoned and regain her citizenship. Yet, having suffered continually from the savaging, sensationalist media, she begged the committee to conduct a low keyed campaign since she always received crank calls as soon as the press reported anything about her. This was a near impossible task since the American public had to be informed to be "reeducated."[29]

At long last, breaks came to help Iva's cause. On 22 March,

1976, the *Chicago Tribune* published a story from their Tokyo correspondent, Ronald Yates, with the headline, "Tokyo Rose's Accusers Claim U.S. Forced Them To Lie." Kenkichi Oki and George Mitsushio admitted: "We had no choice. The U.S. Occupation Army Police came and told me I had no choice but to testify against Iva or else. We were told that if we didn't cooperate, Uncle Sam might arrange a trial for us, too. So we cooperated and we did what we were told and now we have a guilty conscience because of it."[30]

The biggest media break came on CBS' "60 Minutes" program of 20 June, 1976. Morley Safer gently guided her through the interview and also featured the voice of John Mann, foreman of the jury that convicted Iva. Mann stated:

> There was a great deal of anti-Japanese prejudice existing throughout the country, especially here in California. And that had some effect on the jury. Of that I'm quite certain. There have been very few months since the trial that I did not think of her and think that she was not guilty. And I am rather sorry that I did not stick to my guns.

The impact of "60 Minutes" was fantastic. Editorials across the nation were written and letters in support of Iva came pouring in. Veterans across the country began letter writing campaigns and passing resolutions in support of pardoning Iva. Senator Spark M. Matsunaga, a decorated combat veteran of the famed 442d Infantry Regiment, led the campaign to urge the president to pardon Iva.

On 17 November, 1976, the committee, with Iva Toguri present, sent the pardon petition to President Ford from the Federal District Court of San Francisco, the same building where twenty seven years earlier Iva had been convicted. It was timed to be on the president's desk before the year end holiday season because this is the traditional time when presidents favored pardons. Then anxiety mounted day after day as the holiday season approached. Christmas came, no pardon action. New Year's came and passed—still no word. The seventeenth of January arrived and still no action. Iva seemed resigned that, like Eisenhower, Johnson, and Nixon, President Ford would not be pardoning Iva. Only two days remained before President Ford would be out of office. But late in the afternoon of the 17th, a news report from station KCBS stated that the president did intend to pardon Iva on his last day in office, the 19th. The Committee and Iva, having opened a command post in a back room of Toguri Store, were all ears and constantly telephoning the radio and television stations for more definitive news. Bill Kurtis of Chicago's station WBBM reported that White House pardon-attorneys confirmed that President Ford had signed the pardon petition. The legend of Tokyo Rose had finally been destroyed and Iva was to formally regain her coveted American citizenship.[31]

Conclusion

Iva Toguri d'Aquino was a victim of a legend — a legend born of wartime hysteria and of wartime racial prejudice. This essay has shown how she was victimized by U.S. wartime propaganda and the hatred spewed against Japanese Americans during the war and post war period by sensationalist reporters and newspapers, by super-patriot American organizations, and by U.S. government officers. The essay has described the role that racial prejudice played against a victimized, railroaded Japanese American woman — ironically, a young woman who naïvely believed true justice to be automatically bestowed upon any citizen, especially one who continually declared her allegiance and loyalty to America. Tokyo Rose was a myth, a myth that tragically devastated Iva Toguri d'Aquino.

End Notes

1. "*Nisei*" is a Japanese term for those born in America of immigrant parents. It denotes a second generation person, and their children born in America are called "*Sansei*." The first generation (immigrants) are called "*Issei*." These are generational terms and they include cultural values, beliefs and norms particular to the ethnic Japanese.

2. The pre-war Japanese American experience in employment was heavily influenced by discrimination. Professional or supervisory positions in the general business sector were not available to Japanese-Americans, well qualified though they be. College graduates often entered the employment as typists or even as grocery clerks, usually in the cities' "Japan Town." Some even opted to go to Japan to find professional work.

3. Uyeda, p. 5.

4. Duus, pp. 71-73.

5. Duus p. 77.

6. Duus, p.78.

7. Duus, p. 79.

8. Duus, p. 81.

9. Duus, p. 79.

10. Ruth Hayakawa, June Suyama, and Mieko Furuya Oki were other Nisei women who had broadcast the "Zero Hour" programs.

11. Cousens was delighted when Ince told him that 'Lil Orphan Annie' was a popular comic strip character in the United States.

12. The U.S. Navy on 7 August, 1945 issued a citation to Tokyo Rose for her entertaining programs. Veterans, in a survey after the war, indicated that the programs were highly entertaining and not a demoralizing factor (Howe, p. 65).

13. Two other women employed in the broadcasts were Katherine Morooka Reyes and Mary Ishii.

14. Howe, p. 62.

15. This sum was huge and particularly enticing because the exchange rate was 15 yen to a dollar and most Japanese families were living on 100 yen a month at that time.

16. Duus, p.25.

17. Ibid. Carr was later appointed a judge in the U.S. District Court of Los Angeles.

18. Duus, p. 34.

19. Uyeda, p. 7.

20. Uyeda, p.8.

21. Howe, p. 125.

22. National Japanese American Historical Society (NJAHS), p. 14., see Appendix.

23. United States Constitution.

24. Oki's wife, Miyeko Furuya Oki, was also an announcer in the "Zero Hour" program. Both Mitsushio and Oki were one time residents of California and had attended college there.

25. NJAHS, p. 25.

26. Felipe and Iva, despite being strong Roman Catholics, agreed to dissolve their marriage—it was physically impossible for them to continue their marriage.

27. *New York Times*, 29 January, 1959.

28. NJAHS, p. 17.

29. Duus, p. 227.

30. NJAHS, p. 30.

31. NJAHS, p. 17.

Selected Bibliography

"Americans of Japanese Ancestry and the United States Constitution" (San Francisco, CA: National Japanese American History Society, 1987).
Chuman, Frank F., *The Bamboo People* (Del Mar, Publishers Inc.,

1979).

Conroy, Hilary, and Miyakawa, T. Scott, *East Across The Pacific* (Santa Barbara, CA: Clio Press, 1972).

Daniels, Roger, *Concentration Camps U.S.A.* (New York, NY: Holt, Rinehart, and Winston, Inc., 1972).

Duus, Masayo, *Tokyo Rose: Orphan Of The Pacific* (New York, NY: Harper Rowe, 1979).

Gayn, Mark, *Japan Diary* (New York, NY: William Sloan Inc., 1948).

Grodzius, Morton, *Americans Betrayed* (Chicago, IL: University of Chicago Press, 1949).

Hosokawa, Bill, *Nisei: The Quiet Americans* (New York, NY: William Morrow, 1969).

Howe, Russell W., *The Hunt For Tokyo Rose* (Lanham, MD: Madison Books, 1990).

Lee, Clark, *One Last Look Around* (New York, NY: Duell, Sloan and Pierce, 1947).

Meo, Lucy D., *Japan's Radio War On Australia* (Melbourne, Australia: University Press, 1968).

"Nikkei Heritage," Volume VI, No. 3 (San Francisco, *CA::* National Japanese American History Society, 1994).

Ogawa, Dennis, *Jan Ken Po*, Japanese American Printing Center (Honolulu, HA: Obun Printing, 1973).

"The Kibei," Volume III (*San Francisco, CA:* National Japanese American History Society, 1994).

"The Kibei" (Los Angeles, CA: *Pacific Citizen*, December, 1984).

Weglyn, Michi, *Years of Infamy* (New York, NY: William Morrow, 1976).

CHAPTER NINE

JAPAN'S FUGO PLAN: THE BALLOON BOMBING OF AMERICA

Introduction

The purpose of this essay is to describe another of Japan's bizarre tactics of World War II. The Pearl Harbor debacle of December 7, 1941, generated a highly publicized retaliatory venture on the part of the United States. The U.S. government felt the need to buck up American morale, and thus launched the epic air raid of Tokyo and other major cities led by Lieutenant Colonel James Doolittle on 18 April, 1942. To be sure, the raid resulted in minimal damage to the cities and did not affect Japan's war production capacity. But it did shock Japan's military into attempting to retaliate.[1] The wholesale loss of face for her military—they had failed to keep the enemy far away from the imperial environs of Tokyo—was a part of the thinking which led Admiral Yamamoto to plan a strike against the United States at Midway, on June 3 and 4, 1942.

As it turned out, however, the battle of Midway was a devastating defeat for Japan's Imperial Navy and so Midway became the turning point of the war.[2] Japan's military, the Imperial Army staff in particular, began to grope for a way to continue the war against the American enemy. Early on, the Imperial Navy had launched an airplane from the deck of a submarine, on the 9th and 29th of September, 1942, off the coast of Oregon, from which incendiary bombs were dropped into the Siskiyou Forest. However, the bombs failed to ignite and cause a fire in the rain soaked forest. Since the fortunes of war had turned against the Imperial Navy she decided that it was no longer feasible to hazard her submarines and planes in this type of venture. Such were the historical events leading to the Fugo Plan to bomb America by use of balloons.

The Fugo Plan

Japan's Fugo Plan was designed to be an intercontinental weapon—bombs ferried across the wide Pacific in giant balloons, taking advantage of the prevailing winds and the stratospheric jet streams. The incendiary and anti-personnel bombs on the balloon (five in total) were designed to be dropped automatically after being cast aloft for a period of 72 hours, the calculated average time for the balloons to cross the Pacific. Then a second bomb attached to the balloon would explode and destroy the balloon itself, leaving little if any evidence as to the bomb dropping weapon. An irony in this fantastic tactic, the balloon bombing of America, was that it preceded our great fear, rampant during the Cold War, of possible intercontinental missile attacks from the USSR (Union of Soviet Socialist Republics).

Balloons as war weaponry is not new. They were used during our Civil War, especially by the Union forces, to observe an ongoing or projected battle from an elevated vantage site. The Japanese used such observation balloons in their attacks to capture Port Arthur during the Russo-Japanese War of 1904-05. World War I and its aftermath witnessed the introduction of barrage balloons and dirigibles.

Meteorology

As early as the 1920's Japanese scientists were studying the jet stream, which is located about six to twelve miles above the ground, and moving in an east to west direction. The Tokyo Central Meteorological Observatory became the chief authority and repository for their experimental data concerning the wind patterns and jet stream. In the 1930's the Army's 9th Military Technical Research Institute formally tasked the Observatory to conduct experiments to see if the jet stream could possibly be a conveyor of large balloons across the Pacific.

Between 1942 and 1944 facts and data were collected and studied from seven radio sonde[3] stations at Sendai, Niigata, Wajima, Yonago, Fukuoka, Shio-no-Misaka and Oshima. From these stations, as well as from scattered island and ship surface observations across the northern Pacific, they were able to calculate the probable wind flow patterns across the Pacific Ocean. The Observatory found that the jet stream over or south of Japan, at about 9.1 Kilometers (30,000 feet), was particularly strong during the months of November through March and the use of the jet stream in this period would enhance the probability of success in bombing America.[4]

The Balloon Bombs

Buoyed by the Observatory's report, the army put Major General Sueyoshi Kusaba in charge of the program to bomb the American mainland with balloon bombs.[5] Kusaba employed Japan's leading scientists, university aeronautical and meteorological professors, and balloon manufacturers to work on a crash program to build the trans-Pacific balloons. They developed two types of balloons that were to be filled with hydrogen. One was manufactured from paper and the other from rubberized silk. The paper balloons were of two sizes, one 45 feet in diameter and the other, for use in the winter, was 30 feet in diameter. The rubberized silk balloon was about 30 feet in diameter.

The balloons were designed to float at an altitude above 30,000 feet. A problem that had to be solved was that the daytime sun would expand the balloon and cause the sphere to burst. Then, the extremely low temperatures in the evening, from 0° to -500° C. would cause the balloon to lose its altitude and drop out of the jet stream. The Japanese scientists fashioned an ingenious method to keep the balloon at an even keel and desired altitude—they installed a gas discharge valve which would be activated as the balloon ascended too high and in the evening, as the balloon descended too low, out of the jet stream, an automatic device was triggered and a sand ballast would be released, thereby allowing the sphere to stay in the jet stream. The balloon carried thirty two sand bag ballasts and when all ballasts were released, one by one, another automatic device was activated which released all the bombs and this caused instant demolition of the balloon in flight by another explosive charge carried close to the balloon.[6] The balloons were designed to be in flight 72 hours, the maximum time calculated for the flight across the Pacific.

The balloons were ten meters in diameter (32.8 feet) and were made with three or four layers of tissue paper, cemented together to form a gas-escape-proof sphere, filled with hydrogen gas to a capacity of 19,000 cubic feet. The Japanese scientists and technicians enveloped the upper half of this sphere with more layered paper and had a scalloped cloth band attached to the envelope. Then shroud lines were attached to the cloth band and the lines were tied to gondola-like baskets from which the bombs and ballasts were to be released. The large balloons were able to lift 1,000 pounds at sea level and about 300 pounds at 30,000 feet.[7]

Imperial Japanese Navy Balloons

Unwilling to be outdone, the IJN (Imperial Japanese Navy) carried out balloon experiments on their own, initially, later to be incorporated under the aegis of the 9th Military Technical Research Institute, with Major General Sueyoshi Kusaba in overall charge. The navy balloon was categorized as Type B while the Army's was type A. The navy's balloon was constructed of rubberized silk and this proved to be a definite drawback since the weight was considerably more than the Army's papered balloon. Consequently, the Type B naval balloon had to be reduced to 10 meters diameter and its payload was diminished accordingly. Other disadvantages of the Type B balloon emerged: though more durable than the Army's paper balloon the ascendancy was slow and it bounced along the ground before rising and this tended to damage the balloon and its payload, and the shroud lines often became entangled. It took two to two and a half hours for the Type B to reach the fast moving jet stream. On the other hand, the Army's Type A paper balloon reached the 10,000 meter level in forty minutes and carried a heavier payload. Other disadvantages were that the rubberized material for the Type B balloon was difficult to manufacture, and much costlier.[8] In all, only three hundred Type B balloons were manufactured, and these were used principally for weather and experimental purposes.

Manufacture of the Balloons

To minimize damage and time loss in transporting the fragile paper balloons the manufacturing sites were located close to Tokyo where there were paper factories and large high ceilinged or domed buildings (like the Nichigeki Music Hall, Toho Theater, and the Kokugi Kan Wrestling Hall) to paste and gas proof the balloons.[9]

The paper was manufactured from the fibers of the kozo bush, a member of the mulberry tree family, and the sheets weighed 15 grams per square meter. The sheets were joined at the seams by an adhesive made from konyaku-nori, a type of Japanese potato, so wags would often term the balloons as konyaku bombs.[10] The sheets were pasted together and formed three or four overlays placed lengthwise and crosswise for added strength. After the sheets were laminated in order to prevent possible gas leaks, the upper hemisphere of the ballon was formed first, then the lower. The two spheres were then sealed together and an encircling scalloped cloth band was glued on the middle of the sphere and the shroud lines were attached to this suspension skirt. In all, 600 paper panels were needed for a balloon. The balloons were then tested for gas leaks in these large halls or circular shaped buildings. Given the wartime exigencies and materiel shortages it is truly remarkable that the Japanese military and scientific community, along with patriotic civilians, many of them high school girls, were able to produce upwards of 10,000 of these large balloons, all dependent on simple machinery and hand labor.

Launching of the Balloon: The Sites

The Army formed a new unit called the Special Balloon Regiment and selected three sites on the eastern seaboard of central Honshu; Otsu in Ibaraki Prefecture, Ichinomiya in Chiba Prefecture and Nakoso in Fukushima Prefecture. They purposely avoided locating any sites on the island of Hokkaido to avoid any balloons going towards Russian Kamchatka.

Filling the balloon with hydrogen was the most dangerous, especially during high winds, and sites were therefore secluded within or behind hills This proved the most effective in avoiding wind blown accidents. Sites were connected to rail lines in order to readily transport the materials, munitions and gas tanks. The sites had been carefully selected so that they would follow the jet streams on a line following the 40th north latitude, in accordance with General Kusaba's decision to attempt to hit the heart of America.

Artistic rendition of a balloon launching site.

This line generally included Redding, California, Reno and Ely, Nevada, Provo, Utah, Denver, Colorado, and on into the states of Nebraska and Kansas. General Kusaba was advised by his meterologists that the best time to release the balloons was the five month winter period from November through March when the jet streams eastward were the strongest, and the period immediately after the passing of a high pressure front. This period, at its optimum, would include about fifty balloon launching days.

The first balloons were released on 3 November, 1944, and they expected to release a total of 200 balloons per day from the three sites. To prepare and release a balloon required a crew of thirty men. By the end of the war (15 August 1945), despite difficulties, upwards of 10,000 balloons had been released into the jet stream. Of those, perhaps, about a thousand had made the 6,000 mile crossing over the Pacific, but only 285 have been reported by U.S. authorities. Some had travelled inland as far as Michigan, Alberta, Canada and as far north as Alaska.

Security wasextremely tight and all Japanese markings were omitted. Alphabets and numbers were used instead.[11] The launch sites were isolated, so peering eyes or bypassers were kept at a distance. At any rate, the few Japanese located along the coast could not have imagined a weapon of this sort, that could travel all the way across the Pacific to bomb the Americans.

The Bombing of America

It was on 3 November, 1944 that the first transoceanic balloon bomb was released—the most propitious psychological day. It was the birthday of their greatest modern day emperor, Emperor Meiji. Then too, our naval forces were now being battered by a bizarre weapon known as the Kamikaze. Their ally, the Germans, had initiated their V-2 rocket attacks against England and the latter kept the United States in a state of great apprehension, wondering if there could be advanced rocketry to attack America. If the balloons would rain bombs on the cities or interior forest lands, this would certainly cause general panic among the civilians. This was the fondest dream of the Japanese military, a hope, slim at best, that the United States could thus be forced to cease the impending invasion of Japan.

By the end of the war the Japanese Balloon Regiment had released a total of 9,300 balloons.[12] Of these a total of 329 fell on 26 states and the northern and western provinces of Canada. Several drifted as far north as Alaska, one dropped in Hawaii, and several landed in Mexico, but the most numerous were in Oregon where a total of forty two landed.[13] Our Army authorities forbade any publicity for a while, strategizing that the lack of information would deny the Japanese of vital intelligence to aid their bombing program.

Gradually, the news leaked out as more and more incidents occurred across the country and continent. A balloon came down in woods near a ranch in Yerington, Nevada. The surprised rancher, noting that it was a large balloon without any bombs and other devices, called the Nevada Naval Ammunition Depot, but no one was interested. The man cut up the balloon and used the panels as cover for his haystacks.

On 6 December, 1944, a balloon dropped its bombs near Thermopolis, Wyoming, and this naturally shocked the residents. The fragments indicated that the bombs were of Japanese manufacture, but how could this be? How could the Japanese drop a bomb this far inland—all the way into Wyoming? In the same month damaged balloons were discovered in Alaska, and on 31 December, 1944, a balloon was found snagged in a tree near Estavada, Oregon.

On 4 January, 1945, a huge explosion rocked the home of a Medford, Oregon, resident. Not far from the house a huge hole had been bomb blasted. Again, bomb fragments indicated that they were of Japanese origin. On that same day a balloon was recovered at Sebastopol, California, 55 miles north of San Francisco. The fragments and balloon fabrics were sent to the Naval Research Laboratory in Anacostia, D.C., where scientists and bomb experts examined them. Their report:

> It is now presumable that the Japanese have succeeded in design-
> ing a balloon which can be produced in large numbers at low cost

and which is capable of reaching the United States and Canada from the Western Pacific carrying incendiaries and other devices. It must be assumed that a considerable number are coming over.[14]

An American fighter plane even shot down a balloon with its bombs intact near Alturas, California. The Army repaired the bullet holes in the balloon, refilled it with helium and the balloon was as

Map of U.S. showing approximate locations of reported sightings and landings of the Fugo-Plan balloons based on data from the Smithsonian Institution.

good as new. Our military authorities were puzzled and jittery. We did not know how to stop these balloon attacks. Bomb explosions were now being reported from towns, forests, and open fields but fortunately none from populated areas. Sheriffs from towns in Arizona, Colorado, Texas, Utah and Washington were reporting balloons and bomb attacks—even Iowa, Kansas, Nebraska, and as far inland as Grand Rapids, Michigan, sent in reports of balloons and bombs.

However, the complete silence and self censorship of the American public and her media left the Japanese with overwhelming doubts concerning the overall effectiveness of the balloon attacks. As the B-29 attacks increased on Tokyo and without any report emanating from the Americans concerning any results of the balloons or bombings, Japan terminated her efforts in the early part of April 1945.

Tragedy In Oregon

Tragedy struck on 5 May, 1945, when Reverend Archie Mitchell, of Bly, Oregon, and Mrs. Mitchell took five children on an outing. As Reverend Mitchell was moving his car, Mrs. Mitchell and the five children gathered around a strange object on the ground. Even as Mr. Mitchell cried out a warning to leave the object alone, the bomb, disturbed by the children, detonated and immediately killed Mrs. Mitchell and the five youngsters.[15] This sad incident is the only known case of Americans being killed on the American mainland due to enemy action, the only balloon bomb casualty case. In 1949 Congress awarded a total of $20,000 to the victim's families: $5,000 to Mr. Mitchell, and $3,000 each to the five aggrieved families. Congress felt that the military authorities had not warned the American public of the balloon bomb dangers despite knowing that such bombs were evident in the fields, forests, and other areas.

Conclusion

Despite propaganda boasts from Tokyo that a secret weapon, ("something big" is on the planning board to bring victory to Japan) the Fugo Plan was obviously a military failure. It did not turn out to be the revenge-weapon against Colonel Doolittle's raid on Tokyo of April, 1942, nor Japan's anticipated secret decisive weapon. Since intelligence was practically zero for the Japanese concerning the balloons and bombs, they were presumed to have allocated their meagre resources to other forms of retaliation against the Americans. Japan's efforts did cause some amount of worry and concern to our military leaders. In a way, it was a form of psychological warfare thrust upon our leaders.

The tactic that would have caused the greatest distress and disquietude to all Americans and the world would have been a Japan that engaged in chemical and or biological warfare, transporting the agents in these silent, floating giant balloons. Our U.S. government authorities, particularly the military, were immensely concerned with the prospective chemical and biological thrusts that Japan could have engineered. A wholesale scare, a nation-wide panic, would have resulted immediately. The government, deeply cognizant of these possibilities, sagely requested and urged local and national presses and other media to withhold any information concerning the balloons, which they did. Had Japan's Fugo Plan been successful, it would have changed the entire complexity of Japan's second world war efforts against the United States. The U.S. was fortunate that Japan did not succeed in this bizarre attempt to strike back against us.

Fortunately, Japan could not control the vagaries of the free floating balloon as a military weapon. The Fugo balloon campaign was Japan's unique experiment, but in essence, it was a military failure.

Notes

1. Battle of Midway occurred on June 4th and 5th, 1942. Saburo Ienaga, an eminent Japanese scholar wrote (p. 143): "Yamamoto's greatest battle fleet suffered an unprecedented defeat as the carriers *Akagi*, *Kaga*, *Hiryu*, and *Soryu* were sunk. . . . It was a battle designed to save the Japanese military's face."

2. Of six carriers sent into the Battle of Midway, four were sunk by U.S. action. The *Akagi*, *Kaga*, *Hiryu*, and the *Soryu* were carriers that had participated in the attack on Pearl Harbor.

3. "Radio sonde" refers to a compact package of meteorological instruments and a radio transmitter, carried aloft by a small balloon to measure and transmit temperature, pressure and humidity data from the upper atmosphere to ground observers by means of special radio signals, (New York, NY: *Webster's New World Dictionary*, World Publishing Company, 1968).

4. H. Arakawa of the Tokyo Observatory was chiefly responsible in conducting the meteorological experiments (Robert C. Mikesh, p.7).

5. Sullivan, p.23.

6. Mikesh, pp.8-9, Sullivan pp. 24-5.
7. Mikesh, p. 9.

8. Mikesh, p.11. Mikesh reports that the average balloon load was about 50 pounds with a typical maximum bomb load being one 33-pound (15 kilograms) HE (high explosive) bomb, or one 26.4 pound (12 kilograms) incendiary bomb, or four, 11-pound (five kilograms) incendiary bombs.

9. Circular, high-ceilinged buildings were the optimum since pillars and obtrusions in the work area would interfere with the making and inflating of the balloon. All sides of the hall would be carefully wrapped with paper to protect the balloons from being punctured.

10. Mikesh, p. 13.

11. The Japanese military desired absolute secrecy in order to baffle the U.S. as to the origin, nature and future use of the balloon bombs. This was part of a ploy to gain the psychological advantage over the

enemy, the U.S. (See "Balloons of War," The New Yorker, 29 January, 1996, p.59).

12. John Covington, http://www.seanet.com/~johnco/fugo.htm. Some indicate that 10,000 balloons were released by14 August, 1945.

13. Sullivan, p.32.

14. Sullivan, p.28.

References

Covington, John, http://www.seanet.com/~johnco/fugo.htm

Ienaga, Saburo, The Pacific War, Pantheon Books, New York, 1968.

Mikesh, R.C.,"Japan's World War II Balloon Bomb Attacks On North America," (Washington, DC: Smithsonian Institution Press, 1973.

Sullivan, George, Strange But True Stories of World War II, (New York, NY: Walker & Company, 1983).

The New Yorker, "Balloons of War," 29 January 1996, pp. 52-59.

Webster's New World Dictionary of American Language, World Publishing Company, New York, NY, 1968.

CHAPTER TEN

SPADY KOYAMA

T *he following essay is by Colonel (U.S.A. Ret.) Spady Koyama, a Nisei combat veteran and linguist during the Pacific cam- paigns of WWII and also a participant in the Korean War and Vietnam war. He has graciously given permission for his story to be included in this book..*

Spady A. Koyama was born June 1917 in Ferry, Washington, where his father was a section foreman for the Great Northern Railroad. After his father died, Koyama was sent to Japan. Six years later he returned to Spokane where he accepted his uncle's sugges- tion to adopt his father's nickname, Spady, a tribute for being handy with the basic tool of a railroad section gang, the spade. Over the years, the name became Spady. It was legalized in the U.S. Army.

Koyama spent 12 months in hospitals for wounds received during the invasion of the Philippines at Leyte Island. Back in Spokane he received an invitation from the War Department to return to active duty on 27 January 1947 and within months, won a direct commission as an officer. He retired medically on 17 July, 1970, with the rank of colonel. At the time of his retirement, he was a member of the staff and faculty of the Army Intelligence School. Subsequently, his permanent disability adjudication was elevated to 100 percent.

Koyama is a national director of the Army Counterintelligence Corps Veterans, a past three-term (unprecedent- ed) president of the Spokane chapter, The Retired Officers Association (TROA) and later a two-term president of the Washington State Council of 11 chapters, TROA. Since retirement, he has appeared more than 50 times before students at various levels and as a speaker for veterans and civic organizations. Spady Koyama truly personifies the principle of the old Japanese saying, "Yesterday's enemy is today's friend."

His Story

In late June 1994, I received a telephone call at my home in Spokane, Washington, from Satoshi Hirano, an elected Tokyo Assembly member. He had learned of my serious illness and hospitalization, and he told me that he and his wife and two others would like to visit me to report my condition to a mutual friend, Yoshio Takayama. The four were on a vacation trip to Alaska but when Hirano learned of my condition they drove to Spokane, arrived late at night, visited the following morning, took many pictures of me to show to Takayama, and left that same day to drive back to Seattle in order to catch the flight back to Tokyo.

I had entered a hospital in Spokane in May 1994 to check on my World War II shrapnel, a made-in-Japan souvenir, which I received in my chest during the invasion of the Philippines at Leyte Island in October 1944. Within 24 hours after checking into the hospital, I was on the operating table as an emergency case for what turned out to be an eight bypass coronary surgery. While recovering, I suffered two attacks of bleeding ulcers, which required a transfusion of a total of 56 pints of blood. During this time, my wife was summoned to the hospital twice, both times after midnight, as the medics believed that I would not survive. After five weeks in the hospital I was finally released to recuperate at home and to start a closely monitored health exercise program sponsored by the Heart Institute. I was at home and ambulatory when the four Japanese visitors arrived in the morning on their way to Seattle.

Let me now identify Takayama and Hirano.

The New Guinea Tour

In the spring of 1944, I had volunteered out of General MacArthur's Headquarters in Australia to serve with Headquarters 6th U.S. Army. My assignment was to help interrogate Japanese prisoners of war at the newly opened prisoner of war compound at Hollandia in Dutch New Guinea just north of Australia. I interrogated Takayama, an Imperial Japanese Navy petty officer, and noted his fine physical appearance and leadership qualities. We selected him to help us in the management of the camp and in the daily activities, which included roll calls and selection of healthy prisoners to work

Japanese prisoners of war. Takayama is at upper right.
(Photo, courtesy of Spady Koyama.)

outside the camp to clear debris from the surrounding jungle. We were in close contact with each other from that time on. The camp continued to flourish and expand as the number of prisoners continued to increase. At one point, over 500 prisoners were sent down to Australia while Takayama remained behind in Hollandia.

In September, we were ordered to break down our tents outside the compound, as we were leaving for an unknown destination. Takayama approached the fence and stated that he had a final request before I left. He then asked for my name and address to enable him to thank me after the war for the alleged kind treatment extended to him and the rest of the prisoners. I was surprised, but I quickly replied that I could not give him my name and address. He was visibly disappointed. I was not about to possibly jeopardize the safety of my younger brother and two sisters who were still in Japan. I then informed Takayama that if I survived and reached Japan, that I would make an effort to find him inasmuch as I knew his name, rank, and home prefecture.

Near Death in Leyte

On 25 October, 1944 I was aboard the Landing Ship Tank (LST) #552. (To many of us LST stood for Large Slow Target.) It was part of a huge convoy of ships headed to the north for Leyte Island in the Philippines. LST #552 took a direct hit from a *Kamikaze* dive bomber. I was seriously wounded and found myself in the group whose uniforms were cut off except for our shorts, obviously to aid the medics in determining the exact location of our injuries. When I regained my senses some time later, I found myself lying with others on a sandy beach and wondered what my chances were if we were to be strafed by enemy planes. At that time I noted that my hearing was not up to par and that I could not see out of my right eye. I checked my face for my left ear and right eye and noted that I had suffered cuts and burns on my face. After I checked my face with my right arm, I left the arm on my chest. This single act of leaving my arm on my chest when others on both sides of me were laid side by side with their arms at their sides did indeed attract attention. I heard someone call out to a nearby chaplain who hurried over to my side to ask for my religion. Before I could reply, he asked, "Buddhist?" When I shook my head, he looked surprised and looked again at my bloodied identification tag and said, "Looks like a 'B' but

I guess it's a P for Protestant." With that he launched into the recitation of the 23rd Psalm as I lost consciousness again. This is how I escaped being buried along with the others. I was evacuated from there to spend the next 12 months in various hospitals before being discharged from the Army with 40 percent disability. Although I had surgery which required 34 stitches to my chest and the removal of my fifth rib, the main piece of shrapnel still remains lodged in my lung wall.

Medical Discharge and
Reentry Into Service

Back in Spokane in 1946, I was working at the Galena Air Depot, forerunner of the current Fairchild Air Force Base. Since I had security clearance from my assignment in the Military Intelligence activities in General MacArthur's GHQ in Australia, I was promptly assigned to wear a pistol on my right hip and given an assistant to drive down to the main post office in Spokane and pick up all the classified mail for the depot. Since it was less than a year of the end of World War II, my appearance with the weapon in the heart of Spokane attracted some attention, as my assistant and I would stop at the coffee shop across from the post office.

In late 1946, I received an unusual communication from the War Department (Pentagon) which invited me back on active duty by offering a special waiver of my 40 percent disability and the right to return with the highest World War II rank. This meant that I could return to active duty as a technical five-stripe sergeant despite the fact that I had been out of uniform for 15 months. Although my mother hadn't said too much, I knew that the unknown fate of two daughters and a son caught in Japan during World War II preyed on her mind. Without too much opposition from anyone, I went back into the Army in January 1947, exactly five years to the month when I first had to threaten members of the Selective Service Board with a newspaper article before they would process me to Fort Lewis to enter as a buck private to earn $21 a month. Within seven months, I received a direct commission to second lieutenant.

Return To Tokyo

After arriving in Tokyo in 1949, I recalled the promise that I had made in New Guinea in 1944. I visited the Army Demobilization Bureau, a Japanese Government office, and explained my predicament. The official excused himself but returned a few moments later with the bureau chief himself who expressed delight and astonishment that such a story existed between an American and a Japanese. He then requested permission to look for Takayama, although the official headed an Army Bureau and Takayama was a Navy member.

I thanked the official for his interest and left him to start the search for Takayama. Within two days, I had a telephone call from the official to the effect that Takayama had been found. I explained that Takayama did not know my name and that I would visit the official and give him some money that I wanted sent to Takayama for purchase of a round trip ticket to Tokyo. Soon thereafter, I received details regarding Takayama's arrival in Tokyo.

I reached Tokyo Station a few minutes late and noticed the crowd of people in the center of the large waiting room. When I shouldered my way into the center, I suddenly came upon Takayama seated on the floor with everyone gawking at him. Four years after the end of World War II when the remnants of the uniform of the defeated nation were not worn, Takayama had come into Tokyo wearing a Navy cap, a pair of Navy leggings and carrying a Navy rucksack on his back. When our eyes met, there was instant recognition on his part, and tears began running down his face. I hurriedly took him to a nearby store and improved his appearance before taking him to our home in Tokyo. Takayama insisted on staying in Tokyo to work for me, but after about ten days I finally succeeded in persuading him to return home to his family, parents and farm.

Takayama Sends Hirano To Tokyo

Shortly after Takayama's departure, a young man arrived in Tokyo introducing himself as Satoshi Hirano, age 18, a neighbor of the Takayama family. Hirano said that he had been selected to represent Takayama to work for me as long as I was in Japan. When I declined his offer, Hirano flatly stated that he could not return home. I finally secured employment for him in Tokyo to enable him to visit me as often as he wished and report back to Takayama. This arrangement worked out very well. Since that time, Hirano has continued to stay in Tokyo as a permanent resident, has married and has been an elected member of a Tokyo ward assembly for over 20 years.

My Siblings In Japan

As for my younger brother and two sisters, I found them all in fine shape. All had married and had families. My brother had been a sergeant in the Japanese Army and was an instructor in teaching others how to drive small tanks (since he knew how to drive from his days on a farm near Spokane). During the Vietnam conflict, I visited him twice in Japan where he was the coordinator for Japanese mechanics who repaired U.S. planes and helicopters damaged in Vietnam.

Takayama And Hirano's Visit

In 1989, Takayama and Hirano made a visit to Spokane, and this visit was covered by the local newspaper.[1] This event was highlighted by the presence of an American Air Force retired colonel who had been a prisoner of the Japanese after surviving the Bataan Death March. During their visit, my wife and I drove Takayama and Hirano to Idaho and Oregon on short sightseeing trips. During these trips they took many photographs. In response to my question about the photographs, they replied that they were taking pictures of the coun-

Spady Koyama today (center), with Yoshio Takayama (right) and Satoshi Hirano (left). (Photo, courtesy of Spady Koyama.)

try-side to show that there were no houses or buildings in sight as we travelled in a speeding vehicle. They were of the opinion that if the Japanese warlords had made a vehicular trip into our rural areas and had seen for themselves how huge this country is, then there may not have been the instigation of attacks that led to World War II. They both thought it was like a mosquito stinging a giant. They were impressed with the quality of our highways that enabled vehicles to travel at a high rate of speed which resulted in various kinds of insects to be smashed against the windshield in various colors.

The MIS Story

This Takayama/Hirano story is only one of the many episodes of my experience in Japan in which the Japanese people and government officials regarded the MIS (Military Intelligence Service) presence in Japan with respect and esteem. I could also add that such may well be the story of the MIS. There were some 3,000 linguist personnel stationed in Japan during the seven years of the Allied Occupation period. They were scattered from Hokkaido down to Okinawa in practically every Occupation Force unit, organization and establishment. These people served as the language specialists and experts on the Japanese. They were the liaison and contact personnel for every transaction between the Occupation Force and the government, and the people of Japan.

When the Occupation Force arrived, the Japanese were first met by MIS linguists who treated them with understanding and kindness. Their fear turned to relief, antagonism to cooperation and suspicion to friendliness. This situation paved the way for a level of success of the Occupation that was unprecedented in the annals of human history, and eventually for the lasting peace and friendship between the United States and Japan which we still enjoy today.

In the general election in Japan in April 1995, Hirano was elected to his ward assembly for the seventh time. In September 1995 Hirano was the group leader of some ten elected Tokyo officials and aides who visited the United States on a fifteen day fact finding mission that covered California to New York with numerous but short stops along the way. Hirano telephoned to say that he regretted not being able to leave the group to visit Spokane but stated that he hoped he and Takayama would be able to visit Spokane in 1996.

Notes

1. Nappi, 1989

Bibliography

Nappi, Rebecca, "Former WWII Enemies Come Together As Friends In Spokane" (*The Spokesman-Review Chronicle*, November 5,1989).

CHAPTER ELEVEN

"LITTLE SWITCH": A KOREAN WAR NISEI SOLDIER'S STORY

Introduction

*T*he following monologue is the fascinating, true story of a Nisei soldier's experiences during the Korean War, 1950-1953. Susumu ("Sus") Shinagawa was born and raised on the island of Kauai, State of Hawaii, and he volunteered into the United States Army in 1949. After basic training at Schofield Barracks, Hawaii, he was sent to Japan. For about a year he was with the 34th Infantry Regiment, 24th Infantry Division, Sasebo, Japan, serving as a clerk typist. Later he was temporarily assigned to the Eta Jima School Command, near Hiroshima, for training to become a teletype operator.

One remembers that North Korean soldiers crashed across the 38th Parallel into South Korea on 25 June, 1950. This event marked Susumu's entry into a world of hardships, suffering, and tragedies—all far away from his beloved Hawaii. Susumu's story is lengthy and needed to be edited, but the essence of his gripping story is memorialized on these pages. This is the story of a courageous Korean War Japanese American soldier, Susumu "Sus" Shinagawa, in his own words.

His Story

I came back [to Eta Jima] from a short pass [leave of absence] on 30 June, 1950, when the CQ [Charge of Quarters] told me that my sergeant had called and wanted me to return his call. I said, "Thanks, I'll call him first thing in the morning."

I forgot, and because of that, I later became a Prisoner of War (POW), and that nearly cost me my life. During that morning the PA (public address) announcement was made "All men of the 24th must report back to their regiments." The sergeant's call was to inform me that I need not report back since my unit was not on the "call up" list as yet. I was to remain in school.

Sasebo

Heeding the announcement, I left Eta Jima, boarded the train [along with the other soldiers] and headed back to Sasebo. When we arrived there, we were loaded onto trucks and taken straight to the pier. They did not stop to let me off at my company. While waiting at the pier, I saw troops already on board ship. We stood in formation while the Personnel Officer began reading off names. All the names (about 40) were called except mine.

The Personnel Officer looked at me and asked for my name and company. I told him and that I was with the Composite Service Company. He looked at me and said, "ah huh, 4745 Able Company. You are a rifleman." I said, "What? I'm only a clerk typist." He said, "Sorry son, you're *infantry.*" Talk about a classic Shanghai case!

On board ship the army issued me a rifle and items to complete my pack, but no raincoat. They couldn't find boots that would fit me because of my small feet. There were about forty to fifty Hawaii boys in the 34th Infantry Regiment. Fortunately, one of the guys had an extra pair of combat boots which he gave me. [They were] a little big but [they were] better than the dress shoes I had on.

Arrival in Korea

We left Sasebo on the evening of 1 July and landed in Pusan, Korea, early on the morning of the second. The whole area was pitch dark—black-out conditions was the order of the day. With daylight, our under-strength regiment boarded a train and headed north.

Train load after train load of South Korean troops passed us going south. We wondered what the heck was going on, but were not overly concerned. After all, we had been assured that we were to be on police action duty and not combat duty. Also, North Korea, they said, has no Air Force and only about three obsolete tanks.

We got off the train at Pyongtaek and immediately headed toward a hill about a mile or so north of Pyongtaek. The hill was located on the left side of a main road and I guess we were there to secure the road. About a mile or so on the right side of the road was another hill, where K Company was dug in.

It was now the afternoon of 2 July, 1950. We were told to dig fox-holes and camouflage them from the enemy. Then, as I finished digging my foxhole, it rained hard and since I was without a raincoat I got drenched. Then someone pointed to the top of the hill and there we saw the most ridiculous sight. The CO [Commanding Officer] had pitched his tent on the top of the hill for all to see—it stuck out like a sore thumb!

Sus Shinagawa during the Korean War, 1950 (Shinagawa Collection).

On 3 July, the sergeant ordered me to accompany a rifle squad to reconnoiter a village to the left of the hill. He said since I can speak Japanese, I should go as an interpreter. I told the sergeant, "I can't speak Japanese that well." He said, "That's better than nothing."

As we approached the village we saw an elderly Korean. I asked him if he had seen any red soldiers (I didn't know how to say "communist" in Japanese, but knew how to say red). Fortunately, he understood and said he hadn't seen any.

Everything went without incident on our reconnaissance and we reported back to our company. Since I was a replacement, I didn't know anyone in my squad but learned that two Hawaii boys were in our company. I did not get to see them since we left Pusan, and I don't know what happened to them.

Baptism of Fire

On the morning of 4 July, we saw long lines of civilians dressed in traditional Korean white, walking on the main road, going towards Pyongtaek. We thought nothing of it, and watched for at least a half hour or so, until there were none.

Then, in the early morning of the sixth, I heard a loud bang and got up. It scared the hell out of me, for it was my first experience in battle. I saw three American Sherman tanks operated by the North Koreans, firing shells towards Pyongtaek. Why they didn't fire on us, I don't know. Perhaps, they didn't know that we were there. Why didn't we fire back? I suppose we didn't have the type of ammo to knock out the tanks, except for hand grenades, and we were too far away to do any damage. That incident took me by surprise, and I was shaking for awhile. Then we saw mortar fire, with white phosphorus. It was a pretty sight but not a way to knock off tanks. I later found out that was all we had to fight with. Can you believe that?

Eventually the three tanks moved back to their lines and we never saw them again. About an hour later, we saw some movement by the road and opened fire. After a few rounds, we stopped firing. That was the first time I had fired a rifle in over nine months. I don't know whether I hit anything for I didn't have a chance to zero in my rifle. It certainly cooled my nervousness.

Continued Combat Results
In Death and Wounds

We were ordered to retreat because the enemy had us surrounded. Surrounded! How in the world could that happen? We did
not see any communist troops pass us. We were really outsmarted by
the communists. The other day, all those civilians dressed in white
were actually communist troops in disguise. Imagine, they passed
right in front of us. That was how we were surrounded.

While we were retreating, one of our guys was shot in the
thigh. We couldn't determine where the shot came from. While four
soldiers were carrying the wounded, another carried their rifles. Why
the GI with the extra rifles left us to join the rest of our company is a
mystery. Now that left us with four rifles and I had one of them.

As we were walking toward a village, the enemy opened fire
on us. We dove to the ground on the opposite side of the road and
fired back. I fired about four rounds when my rifle jammed. I tried
kicking the bolt, but it didn't help, so now we had only three working rifles. I guess between the four of us, we must have killed the
enemy, for it got quiet and we began to move again.

We came to a granary and decided to rest. Someone checked
on the wounded person and to our surprise, he was dead. The wound
didn't seem fatal, but I guess he died of shock.

While we were contemplating what to do, a Korean civilian
ran toward us and told us that the communists were coming. By then
we saw the enemy coming toward us. We hurried into the granary,
and hid behind bags of rice which were stacked. The communists
knew we were in there, and threw some hand grenades and opened
fire with their burp guns. All of a sudden, I felt my right arm being
thrown back, but my right arm was not where it should have been. I
thought, "Oh, my god! My right arm was blown off." But when I
looked back, it was still there in an awkward position. Instinctively,
I pulled my arm back to the normal position and placed it between
the buttons of my shirt to serve as a sling. Through all of this I don't
remember feeling any pain. We didn't have a chance to fire back
since we had only three rifles among the eight of us. We came out
and surrendered.

I Become a POW

I felt depressed and I thought this would be my last day on earth. If you know the history of Korea, the Japanese empire ruled Korea for fifty (sic) years and the Koreans hated Japanese for that. To my surprise they treated me just like they treated the other seven soldiers. Perhaps they didn't realize who I was, and for that I am grateful. As we were walking out, I didn't realize that I also got shot on my upper right leg, just above my right knee. It was a clean wound where the bullet passed through. Fortunately, it didn't hit any bone, and I can count my blessings for that. I wouldn't be alive today had it struck a bone, which would have crippled me. Bear in mind, any one unable to walk had a good chance of being shot.

I was lucky in a way, that both of my wounds didn't bleed much. The only first aid treatment I received was from my first aid kit—sulfur and bandages. For the next five or six days that was all the treatment I had on my arm and leg.

Our captors took us to a village where we were joined by fourteen others who were captured before us. They interrogated us and wanted to know why we came to Korea and all that bull.

After the interrogation, they marched us to a railroad track where we thought they were going to shoot us. You have no feelings at this point and just accept anything that comes. I didn't see or notice any of us crying or begging for our lives. We were no heroes, maybe we were too numb at that time to realize the seriousness of the situation. They didn't shoot us. Instead we began marching north. Being of Japanese ancestry, and knowing how much hatred the Koreans had for us, I was fearful for my life, but faith was on my side.

The March North

You will not believe this, but our captors were not too intelligent. As an example, before marching us to the railroad tracks, they lined up all the people with black hair (Mexicans, Italians, Indians, and, of course, Japanese) on one side, and on the other side, all others with red, blond and brown hair.

"You all are Japanese," pointing to us with black hair, and "the others are Americans." Try to explain to them that we were all Americans? No way. This explains why they didn't shoot me when I was first captured.

We started to march northward with our hands tied behind our backs, except for me. At least they understood my predicament and left my injured arm in the shirt. This was 6 July, 1950, and we had been marching for about three to four hours when darkness fell. They put us in a jail house with wooden bars, just like the ones we saw back home in the old Japanese Samurai movies where they imprisoned the bad guys. My arm and leg didn't hurt too much the first night, and I was really grateful for that.

The next morning, my arm felt all right, it didn't hurt, but it was beginning to swell and was changing color. My leg was stiff, and every time I took a step, it really hurt. Not 'till I walked for a while did the pain go away. It was a very hot and humid day and we were dying of thirst, but the guards would not give us any water to drink. Being wounded made me doubly thirsty. We walked on the banks of the rice paddy which had water on both sides. It was really tempting to jump in to get our fill, but the guards would not let us.

Suddenly, an American jet flew by. The guards ran in the rice paddy to hide. This was our opportunity to dive into the rice paddy to drink the polluted, dung filled water, but who cared. Quenching our thirst was the main concern. For the uninformed, people in the Far East, use human waste to fertilize their crops. That is the kind of water we drank and we would suffer the consequences later on. After the jet left the area, the guards rounded us up and moved us along.

I was in the last group, marching single file on the banks of the rice paddy. A lieutenant was about three feet ahead of me. For no apparent reason, this guard shoved the lieutenant off the bank. The lieutenant with his hands tied behind him tried to brace himself so that he wouldn't fall into the rice paddy. This guard then opened fire at the officer with his burp gun. I could see blood gushing out of his body and he just dropped right there. With no remorse whatsoever, this guard pushes me to keep going. My leg is giving me a lot of trouble, and hurt every time I took a step. My arm was getting worse from the compound fracture and I had no medication to ease the pain. The guards told us that if anyone lagged behind, they would shoot us!

It was about high noon and I was getting really frustrated. I began to have feelings of suicide. I thought to myself, to hell with this life, and knowing that they would shoot me if I lagged behind— so be it!

I couldn't walk fast and felt really miserable. I could see that the others were putting distance between me, and I was anticipating a bullet through my head. This would relieve me of my suffering. I heard a shot and to my surprise, I was still standing. I looked back just in time to see a South Korean soldier drop. He took the bullet which I thought was meant for me. Suddenly, something in my mind made me want to live again. I do not know where I got the strength, but somehow I caught up with the rest of the guys.

Arrival in Anson—Dysentery

It was early evening when we entered a city called Wonson (sic), probably Anson,[1] about 22 miles from where we were captured. The people were lined up on the street, jeering, and spitting on us as we walked through the city. One young soldier came up to me and spoke in Japanese, "I'm going to shoot you." Feeling miserable, I told him, "Go ahead and kill me."

Remember the rice paddy water that we drank? Now I was coming down with dysentery. Here we were in the center of a city and people lined up to see us. I wanted to defecate in the worst way and remembered the guards warning about stepping out of line and getting shot at. I didn't care about the consequences for I still had my pride and would not defecate in my pants. I broke rank and went down an embankment, took my pants off, and defecated while hundreds of people watched. I guess to them it was no big deal, for they do it anywhere they please.

We stayed in Wonson (sic), probably Anson, for three days, and of the 22 Americans captured on 6 July, four [of us] were left behind. Why? I do not know. We were put on a truck headed for Yongdongpo. I was glad for I don't think that I could have kept up with the rest of the guys. My arm had gotten really swollen and I think I was coming down with a fever. The whole arm turned purple, and I was afraid that gangrene might have set in. We arrived at Yongdongpo, where we joined another group of prisoners, which brought the total to about 150. This is where I saw the first Hawaii soldier, but I did not know him. We only made eye contact and acknowledged each other by moving our chin up and down like saying, "Howzit, brother."

We Reach Pyongyang

We left Yongdongpo by train and reached Pyongyang, the capital city of North Korea on 11 July [1950]. They made us march through the city with the lead guys carrying banners. It was hot and humid and I was about in the middle of the group, walking four abreast. I kept up for about a quarter of a mile, and this time, I really had a fever. I had gone six days without any kind of medical treatment. My leg was miserable, it hurt every time I took a step. Finally, I just gave up, and fell to the ground. No one could do anything for me, they just passed me by. My morale at this time was the lowest of all, my pride was broken, for I urinated in my pants and again anticipated a bullet to my head.

Then out of nowhere, another Hawaii soldier from Maui, whom I didn't know, came to my aid. I told him to leave me alone, to go with the rest of the guys or they would kill him too. He said, "Nah, they won't." I had tears in my eyes and again told him to go, but he stayed with me. While a guard stood by us, an officer in a jeep came by and spoke to the guard. The guard must have told the officer of my condition. He looked at me. I must have looked pathetic. He then motioned for me and my new friend, to get into the jeep. We rode all the way to our destination, a POW camp, which was a two story wooden building. It must have been a school with a big yard in front of the building. There we joined another group of prisoners which brought the total to about 750. The guys that were captured with me on the 6th of July helped me to the second floor, and like a baby, I curled up in a ball.

Medical Aid For A POW — Hospitalization

We had an American doctor, captured with another group, who was to check my wounds. When the doctor came, his facial expression told me I was really in trouble. He looked at my arm and leg, and began talking to someone at his side. I didn't know who the other guy was, but I assumed he must be the ranking officer of our group. Later the doctor spoke to an English speaking Korean officer and in all probability told him that I must go to the hospital.

They took me downstairs to a jeep and I went to a hospital not too far from the school. This was a civilian hospital, and for a hospital, it had lots of flies. In the operating room they put me to sleep with ether. When I awoke my arm and leg were heavily bandaged.

For four days, they didn't change my bandages. Soon, I noticed lots of wiggly worms on my bed and felt something moving under the bandages. I took a peek, and saw "millions" of worms in my wounds. It really shook me up, and I got worried. I called for a doctor, and when he came he asked, "What's the matter?"

I said, "There's millions of worms in my wound."

He took off my bandage and I was horrified to see so many worms all over my wounds. I could see three cuts on my arm which had lots of worms. I didn't know what they were until the doctor said,"Very good. They are maggots and they eat all the pus." He scraped off the maggots and sure enough, there was a clean wound. He stuffed the wound with gauze and bandaged it—that's it, no stitches, or anything else.

The biggest cut was at least one inch wide by one-half inch deep by five inches long. As for my leg wound, they stuffed a gauze from each end of the opening where the bullet penetrated my thigh, until they met in the center, then bandaged it. They told me that this procedure made the healing process work from the middle and eventually pushes the gauze out on both ends. I told them that in America we changed the bandage every day. He said, "That method is old fashioned." Here they changed the bandage every fifth day. I can't argue, for it worked. Although it took longer, it healed from the middle.

While I was in the hospital, there was an air raid warning. They took me to an open area outside the hospital, where most of the ambulatory patients were assembled, not to an air raid shelter. I could see our B-29 bombers, with their bomb bays open. That was the most frightening sight, for you knew that the bombs would be falling to earth real soon. The bombs fell all around the hospital but not one came close to us.

Back To The Prison Compound

After two and a half weeks in the hospital, I was sent back to the prison compound. Knowing that I had a compound fracture on my arm, they did not put my arm in a cast. Again, I don't know why.

At the compound, I was feeling better. I also met some guys from Hawaii. The first guy I saw at Yongdongpo was from the 19th Regiment, 24th Division. He was from Honolulu. His name is Goichi Tamaye. The second guy, he stayed with me when I couldn't walk, was from the same regiment as Tamaye. He was from Maui and his name is Tomio Tadaki. I also met Henry Arakaki, from Honolulu, and "Mike," a Japanese national, who was captured about the same time as Tamaye and Tadaki. How Mike ended up as a POW is another story. Anyway, while in Japan, the U.S. Army hired Japanese nationals to do KP [kitchen "police" work] and other duties. Mike was hired as a KP helper. He understood more English than he could speak. When the army unit he worked for was ordered to go to Korea, he somehow managed to go along with them. When the Commies overran the unit, he was captured with the rest of them. Since the Koreans could not speak Japanese, Mike was used as a translator for the American POW's. He really had a rough time when he was first captured, and was threatened with death many times.

One day, while walking around the compound, despite a fever, I came across a buddy of mine from the 34th Regiment. We couldn't say, "Hey, it's nice to see you." Not in our situation. I asked him what happened to the other guys. He told me one of them got killed and didn't know what happened to the rest of the guys because he, himself, was captured. There were at least a dozen or so soldiers from Hawaii; five Japanese, one Korean, and some Hawaiians and Portuguese. Only four Japanese from Hawaii survived and Mike made it too.

Arm Amputation?

My high fever left me weak and listless. Someone called the American doctor. When he saw me, he knew what was causing the fever. He talked to the camp commander and told him that I had to go to the hospital because my arm was getting infected. At that time I could barely move my fingers. The commander ordered his officer to take me back to the hospital and to tell the doctor to have my arm amputated.

When we reached the hospital, the officer told the doctor what the camp commander told him. The doctor examined my arm and told me to move my fingers, which barely moved. He said there was no need to amputate my arm and that he could save it. The officer argued with the doctor and told him that the commander said to amputate. The doctor was reluctant to operate, and so the officer went back to the camp to inform the commander of the doctor's refusal to amputate. The officer later returned and told the doctor to save my arm.

That was one doctor I really respected. There was another GI, who had his right hand amputated, and had a beautiful skin graft over his stump. There was another GI who seemed to have had a butcher for a doctor. One night while the prisoners were sleeping, a guard downstairs was playing with his rifle. It went off, and the bullet went through the floor and hit this GI in the thigh. They took him to a hospital (not the one that I was in) and amputated his leg right above his knee. I got to see him much later when a Korean nurse was changing his bandage. What I saw made me sick. When the nurse took off the bandage, he was holding his thigh with his hands. I could see the red meat with the bone in the middle of it. It looked like a ham shank. The bone was sticking out about an inch because his flesh had shrunk. He was in great pain when the nurse treated his wound around the bone. The doctor who amputated his leg didn't put a skin graft over it. That poor soldier didn't last too long, for he died about a week later. I thought it was most merciful.

They finally put a cast on my arm but didn't use any padding, especially the area under my shoulder. The cast kept rubbing my shoulder for three months, and it was painful whenever I moved my arm.

One morning there was an air raid and bombs were falling all around the hospital. They did not evacuate anyone, so I stayed in bed looking up at the ceiling. Then it happened. A bomb hit the far end of the hospital and the whole building shook. Here, I was in bed looking up at the plaster ceiling and saw the ceiling bouncing up and down. All of a sudden a huge piece of plaster started to fall. I turned and dropped to the floor just as the plaster fell on the entire length of my bed. Before the bombing incident, they used to feed me soup, rice and a side dish. After the bombing, all they gave me was rice. I don't blame them for being angry.

Moved Again—Close To Manchuria:
Life In POW Camp

On 5 Sept., 1950, we boarded a train for a slow journey to Monpo, a little town near the Manchurian border. We arrived there on the eleventh of September. We were quartered in a compound consisting of several long buildings with wooden platforms. Of course, there were guards patrolling the area. There was another small building which served as a hospital for the sick and wounded.

We had an American doctor, but he couldn't do too much because he had no medical equipment, only bandages and gauze. I was his patient and also his interpreter.

We had lots of freedom there. The set up was good. An officer was in charge. We cooked our own meals and ate "cafeteria" style. The food was poor, but we didn't complain, with this kind of set up, why should we? Civilians brought us rice, turnip, *won bok*, and green onions in an ox cart. We did what we had to do without any orders from the guards. The guards came only at night to take a head count.

One night, Tadaki and I were sitting on a platform in the open field with a big moon shining above. We were "shooting the bull" when a Korean guard approached us and tried to make small talk with us in Japanese. He looked, pointed to the moon and asked us if we have a moon in America. We looked at each other and wanted to bust out laughing. Instead, Tadaki, with a serious face said, "In America the moon is blue."

The guard said, "Oh!" and walked away. Remember the incident with black and blond hair? Same, very low intelligence.

Lice is another creature that I hadn't seen before. In Korea, especially in the countryside, it is a common thing with farmers. Lice are found everywhere and some even found their way into my cast. I had no way to get them out. The itchiness was unbearable and at times torturous.

Now it was time to take off my cast. They tried using a knife, a saw, or any available tool but to no avail. Finally, I soaked it in hot water and peeled off the cast layer by layer. The wounds were healed except for one. There was tissue sticking out of the skin and would not heal. I had to keep it bandaged for thirty three months.

We're Moved Once Again

On 19 October, 1950, we departed Monpo, moving south to a small village of Kosan (that's where we saw the first Chinese Red soldiers, crossing the Yalu River). Our next stop was another small village nearby called Danakon. It was at Danakon where we heard artillery fire, and saw the first North Korean wounded coming home. Our hopes shot up, for we felt sure liberation was not far away. However on 26 October, 1950, we were on the move again. This time they separated the sick and wounded, about a dozen of them, from the main group.

I was ordered to stay with the sick and wounded because they needed an interpreter. We rode an ox cart, since most of them could not walk a long distance. We caught up with the main group on the 31 October., in a corn field. They were there for four nights, probably waiting for us to catch up with them

Up to this time we were under the control of the North Korean Army, but that soon changed. We were transferred to the North Korean "Police Force." They were a fanatic and sadistic group that would kill anyone without reason. Coincidentally, this all happened on 31 October, Halloween day. Until then we didn't know how lucky we were to be controlled by the North Korean army.

One day at a bull session, someone heard a rumor that General MacArthur had promised the "boys" they would be home for Christmas. Our morale shot up and there was that feeling of lightness among us with thoughts of liberation. I don't know how that rumor reached us, but it did. Our thoughts of liberation were short lived. We were told that we would be going to another camp northeast of Monpo, about 160 kilometers away called Chunggang Jin.

The Tiger Death March

Before the march began, they divided the group, fifty men to a company, with an American officer in charge. There were about 700 of us, so we had about fourteen companies. They told us that they demanded strict discipline from all of us. If a man should fall behind, the officer must assist him or the officer in charge would be shot. To prove how serious they were, they picked out one officer and shot him in front of us. They repeated, if anybody should fall back, he would be shot. This was no idle threat — this was the beginning of a horrible nightmare.

This was the beginning of our "tiger death march." We had about a dozen civilians, mostly French, and a Catholic priest who were captured in Seoul. This priest, who spoke fluent Korean, was our interpreter during the march. The Korean terrain was terrible, nothing but big mountains and valleys. The five of us who were of Japanese ancestry were used as interpreters. Since I was just released from the hospital, I was put in the first company where I set the pace for the rest of the companies.

One time we were three quarters of the way up a mountain when I looked back and saw the last three of four companies literally running to catch up. Here I thought that we were going slowly. It's like playing a game in the skating rink called "whip." Everyone would hold hands and when it was time to make a turn, the person in the center would take two steps while the end of the whip needed to take five or more steps just to keep up. That's just what was happening. I told the officer to slow down, but the guards would push us on. Every so often, we would hear a rifle shot, and some poor American would not see home again.

At night we slept in the corn fields, huddled in a bunch to keep warm. This was in November, and the winters in Korea are devastating, especially for our group. We were captured during the summer months and had only our fatigues. The Koreans issued us some winter clothing, a quilted cap and either a quilted jacket or quilted pants. I got a quilted jacket. The only thing we had to eat was whole dry corn grain, which was boiled until they became fluffy. We stopped only long enough to fill our caps with it and would start walking and eating at the same time. Naturally, when you are on this kind of diet it would go right through you and make you want to defecate. One of the guys did just that; he broke rank to defecate—he wasn't able to get out of his squatting position before they shot him. The Catholic priest went up and down the column to warn everyone what had happened and told us, under no circumstance, "*do not break ranks!*"

Death March Horrors

From then on, it was a pathetic and sorrowful sight. We ate as we marched. Many ate and marched and defecated in their pants at the same time. It was a miracle that most of us survived the nights. I said "most," because the guy next to you might never wake up; for during the night he could have frozen to death. How could this happen? The day before, we walked, ate the same food, had the same type of clothing, and yet he froze to death. It's a mystery to me.

There was another incident which I was not proud nor happy to hear about. We are Americans and should try to help each other as best we can. We had an airman who was shot in the leg. He walked with his crutches for two days, kept up with us and did not cause any problems. The morning of the third day this "fly boy" could not find one of his crutches. We were ordered to fall in with our company, and began walking. For a while. the airman was able to keep up with us, using only one crutch. Later, he had a hard time doing so and slowly fell back. Finally, a guard came by and shoved him out of the column. He begged the American officer to let him continue. The officer tried to help him, but the guard pushed the officer ahead. Later, we heard a shot and could only guess what happened. How this airman lost one of his crutches made me sick. One of the soldiers got cold at night and burned the crutch to keep warm. Only the strong and the coward survive.

Death March Ends: Life At Chunggang Jin

19 November, 1950: Chunggang Jin . . .

The Lord is my shepherd, I shall not want.
He maketh me to lie down in green pastures.
He leadeth me in the path of righteousness for His name's sake.
Yea, though I walk through the valley of death, I will fear no evil.
For thou art with me.
Thy rod and staff, they comfort me . . .

This is my recollection of the prayer which was given by a Catholic priest. After nine days of hard marching, we could account for 103 soldiers either shot or frozen to death. A majority of them were shot for not being able to keep up. It's not that we didn't try to help each other. We tried our very best to help but the guards would push us along and force us to leave the weak behind. This march was devastating for many of us. During the march, many were frost bitten, had dysentery, pneumonia and other kinds of illnesses. One of the victims was my friend from the 34th Regiment who died from frost bite. Another soldier from Kona, Hawaii, who was in the same regiment as Tamaye and Tadaki, contracted some kind of disease and died after the march. Ironically, both of these guys were boxers for their respective regiment. By the way, Tamaye was also a boxer. When we started the death march, there were about 700 Americans, about 590 survived.

I was in a group of 400 who were quartered in a school-like building. The rest of the guys were in village huts, which had been taken from the villagers. When the guard found out that I could speak Japanese he ordered me to the kitchen detail as an interpreter. I told him that I could speak only a little Japanese. He then asked me if I was Japanese. I told him, "Yes." Then he blew his top. He slapped my face and kicked me. "*bakayaro, nihonjin de nihongo ga wakaran no ka?*" he screamed at me. Translation: "You fool. A Japanese, and you don't know the Japanese language. What do you mean?"

Following that incident, I was more careful how I answered them. If my answers to any of their questions showed a lack of understanding of the language, another beating was in store for me. But my Japanese was really poor. The beatings made it necessary for me to learn Japanese fast, if I was to avoid those unnecessary slaps and kicks from the guards. I picked up the language fast during the months following the first beatings.

Food and Housing

Our first meal at Chunggang Jin was *won bok* soup and millet. Imagine the kitchen crew with twelve heads of won bok, using it to make soup for 400 people. It was winter, and the twelve heads of won bok were frozen solid. We had no knife to cut the cabbages. The only thing that I saw was an ax in the corner of the kitchen and we used it to chop the cabbages. That's all we had, no salt, "no nothing." I was not surprised. We were used to very little food. I broke the news to the boys telling them what they were going to eat. There was nothing they could do or say. We washed the very untasty, boiled millet down our throats with thin cabbage broth. If you got one little piece of cabbage, you were fortunate. At least the broth was hot on this cold winter night. I don't know how the others fared.

During the winter of 1950, rice became scarce and our staples consisted mainly of millet, sorghum grain, and corn. When I first saw millet, I thought of what we fed our chicks at home. But the sorghum grain was worse. It smelled like kerosene.

Later, 400 of us were placed in huts around the village. The huts were about twelve feet wide by 40 or so feet long. The hut was divided into four sections, one end was the kitchen, and the other three were bedrooms or living rooms. The kitchen floor was about four feet lower than the bedroom floor. From the kitchen they dug a trench about a foot wide and six inches deep which ran through the center and the full length of the hut. This trench also branched into each bedroom. The floor was made of mud. As a matter of fact, the whole hut was built with straw and mud. The roof was covered with straw.

The reason why the kitchen floor was lower than the rest of the house made sense. In the center of the kitchen they had a platform made of mud and a big wok. Under the wok, they built a space to burn wood to cook their food. While the wood was burning the heat would enter the trenches to heat the mud floor. That is how they kept themselves warm during the winter. However, during the summer it could become very warm, or even hot.

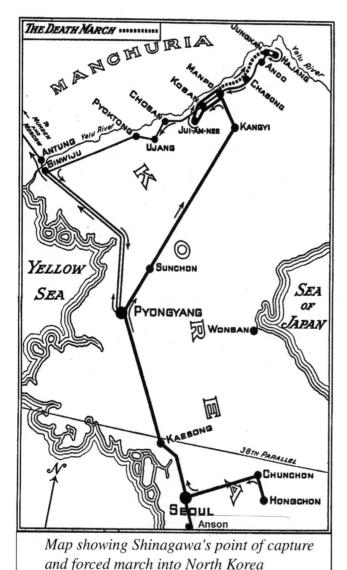

THE DEATH MARCH ••••••••••••

MANCHURIA

Yalu River

MOKPO

Yalu River

TO ANTUNG AND MUKDEN

ANTUNG

SINWIJU

PYOKTONG

CHOSAN

UJANG

JUI-AM-NEE

KOSAN

MANPO

JUNGKAN

HAJANG

ANDO

CHASONG

KANGYI

YELLOW SEA

K

SUNCHON

PYONGYANG

WONSAN

SEA OF JAPAN

R

KAESONG

38TH PARALLEL

N

CHUNCHON

HONGCHON

SEOUL

Anson

Map showing Shinagawa's point of capture and forced march into North Korea

They had straw mats throughout the bedroom. If you were in the first room, next to the kitchen, the floor would get really hot, so hot that sometimes you could not sit there. In the second room, it was real comfortable and in the third room, you could freeze to death, for it took a while for the heat to get there.

We were placed in the huts. We had thirty people in a room nine feet by twelve feet. We were not able to lie down, so we had to sit with our legs folded in front of us. It was very uncomfortable so we took turns stretching our legs. I wouldn't say we had a pleasant night but you can bet your life that there was a lot of grumbling going on. Then too, there were guys who grumbled more than the others. It's a wonder we didn't have a fist fight, for that would have made the guard real happy to see the Americans fighting one another.

Daily Life In the Chunggang Jin Camp:
"Anybody Dead?"

The next day, they issued us cotton padded jackets and pants, which were full of lice. It was an uncomfortable feeling to put on something like that, but it was cold. We had to delouse ourselves every day by taking off our clothes and hunting down the lice in the seams of the jackets and pants. We could feel the lice crawling over our body which made us itchy. Like everything else, we got used to it. On a typical day, we would go outside to stretch our legs, but couldn't stay long for it was too cold.

In every room, there would be at least two or more GIs who would just give up and wouldn't delouse or exercise. They would just lie down and didn't do anything to help themselves. We would force them to get out and move about. We would even go to the extreme and physically throw them out to get their blood to circulate. Time after time they would just crawl back to their little corner wishing to die. They soon had their wish and died shortly.[2]

Day in and day out we saw so many die that we became experts in predicting when a particular person was going to die. It may sound cruel, but most of that person's possessions, even before he died, would be reserved for someone who needed a particular item. As mentioned earlier, we knew when a person was going to die.

Mind you, many of the prisoners were not sick at all. They just gave up. The so called Korean medics used to come by every day and shout, "Anybody sick?" Another thing, whenever anyone died we would place the dead body outside the room. After a week, the medics would come around and yell, "Anybody dead, anybody dead?" I really don't know how many GIs died that winter of 1950. It must have been in the hundreds.

Diseases and Worms

Dysentery was something that we all dreaded; it can get you at any time. You might be healthy today, and the next day, you can catch it. Seems like there was no medication here to treat it. Yet, if we were at home a simple medication could stop it. In Korea, there was no miracle medicine like that. If you have a toothache or earache, you have to just suffer through it, until it goes away. Of course, it might take a few days or even a week for the pain to disappear. I have seen many with severe dysentery, who had to use the toilet quite frequently. Some just left their pants off since it was humbug to keep putting them on and taking them off. I've also seen guys running to the toilet with cotton stuffed in their rectum. You may think it's funny, but it can be a deadly disease. Many suffering from this disease became discouraged due to lack of medication so that they just gave up and died. After days with a bout of dysentery, and when one day you can make a big, healthy fart and nothing comes out, that is when you would see the biggest, happiest smile on any man's face. It is one of the biggest triumphs for a man, for you know you will live to see another day.

In Japan we were warned not to eat raw vegetables or drink well water while in Korea. Somehow, once in Korea under our circumstances we just ignored that warning. We did not get sick from eating raw vegetables but we developed worms. Yes, worms, like earthworms we used to see when you started a garden. The only difference is that the worms we had in our stomachs were pure white. Whenever you defecated, a big glob of worms would come out in a ball. As soon as it hit the ground they would spread out in every direction. There would be at least a dozen or more in each ball, the longest about seven or eight inches long. It really made you sick, when you first experienced it. Some of the guys would have so many worms in them that it would come out of their mouths.

We're Moved Again

We departed Chunggang Jin on 16 November, 1950 and arrived at Hanjang-Ni which was further north on the same day. We departed Hanjang-Ni on 29 March, 1951 and went to Andong where we stayed until 9 October, 1951.

Sometime in July of 1951, an English speaking Red police officer had told us that truce talks were going on. Later, we learned that we were to be transferred to the Chinese forces. These two things got our interest up again. "This is it," everybody was saying. There were all kinds of rumors. One of them had [us being] turned over to the Chinese who would take us back safely to our lines. We waited and waited for things to get started, then, sometime in October, we started to move.

We're Transferred to the Chinese,
Given Pure White Rice!

In July of 1950, when we were gathered in Pyongyang, there were approximately 750 POWs. In October, 1951, there were only 268 of us to be transferred to the Chinese. We were divided into two groups. One group of able bodied men, about 170 of us, were to march 40 kilometers down the Yalu River. We were each given a ball of rice for supper. The other group, the sick and wounded (98) would board a boat at a landing on the Yalu and would meet up with us. The 98 men were squeezed into a boat whose capacity was 85 people. Everyone had to sit. There was no room to move about. It was a weary five day boat trip down the Yalu.

At night, we slept at some village along the river. The last day, it began to rain and sleet. We got all wet, even though there were straw mats to cover our heads. It was very cold. A mile and a half down the river the boats finally arrived and turned into an inlet on the Korean side where we got off.

On 19 October, 1951, we marched another mile and a half to Changson Camp number 3, dripping wet. The Chinese put some of us in huts and the rest in big rectangular buildings, made of straw and mud. I was in a hut with Tadaki, Tamaye, and Arakaki. We were issued an overcoat for the night. It was brand new, so we got rid of our lice infested cotton pants and jacket. They fed us pure white rice. Under the Koreans we never did get pure white rice. It was always mixed with corn and made into a ball, but this, it was unbelievable. We stuffed ourselves, and still had lots of extra rice. Thinking that this would be the only time they would feed us pure white rice, we filled our bowl full of rice for the next morning. When morning came, they brought us another bucket full of pure white rice.

The next day they issued us brand new comforters and cotton padded uniforms. Under the Koreans, we were not allowed to write or receive any mail from home. I strongly believe that had we received some mail from home, many who died would have survived. Word from home would be a goal to live for.

Psychological Persuasion (Brainwashing) Under The Chinese

The Chinese encouraged us to write home and many did just that. I, for one, thought that since my mom had not heard from me for fifteen months probably thought I was dead. Why give her hope again? For that reason I refused to write home. But once the guys' families started to write back and send pictures, that did it! I got homesick and began to write home.

Many were sent pictures taken in front of a car or home and they would show them to our instructors. These instructors were the elite of the Chinese troops. They could all speak English, and tried to brainwash us. The instructors would look at the pictures and say, "This is propaganda pictures. The U.S. Government provides the cars and homes and makes the family stand in front of them." This came from the elite of the Chinese troops!

I remember one session we had, where our head instructor was telling us so proudly, how advanced the Chinese people were becoming. "Now in China," he said, "every other family owns a bicycle." We all laughed but the instructor couldn't see what was so funny. We told him that in America, every other family owns a car, and many families own two or more cars. He was flabbergasted and said, "You are all wrong. The American people are starving and there is not enough food to go around." That is what they were told and that is what they wanted us to believe, that the Americans were starving.

During our "reverse brainwashing talks," we told the instructors that the Americans were not starving and we indeed owned our cars and homes. The instructors were confused. After a while, they stopped giving us lectures.

Further Reflections On My Wounds

Now, let me go back to the time when I was wounded in July, of 1950. In the winter of 1951, a piece of bone worked its way up to my elbow. It became infected. My arm would swell and the skin would stretch so thin that it looked transparent. It would throb for weeks and I could not sleep. Finally, I went to see a Chinese doctor. He looked at my elbow and decided to make an incision to let the pus flow out. It worked! The swelling went down and the pain was gone. He took out a piece of bone and then proceeded to probe into the wound. Mind you, no injection to numb my arm. The pain was unbearable. He kept pulling on another piece of bone but it kept slipping off. He tried many times without success and to my relief, he finally gave up. I thought that was bad. What he did next was worse. He swabbed the wound with iodine. I cannot tell you the pain I was in. Was I ever glad to leave that office. I swore that I would never go back to see him again.

There were times when this situation would repeat itself but I refused to see the doctor. I knew that sooner or later a piece of bone would penetrate the skin and I could pull it out myself. I knew the pus would ooze out, and the swelling and pain would go away. This happened about every three months and I took out several pieces of bone. While being a POW for 33 months my wounds did not heal.

When I was repatriated in 1953 the doctors at Tripler Army Hospital treated my wounds. In three months those wounds were completely healed.

We were still waiting for the good news—liberation! However none was forthcoming for they told us later that truce talks were not turning out well and that we had to stay a while.

Chinese Try Their Xu Xi (Hsu Hsi)[3] Method On POWs

One night in late October, 1951, while a head count was being taken, they [our Chinese captors] mentioned something about schooling. The next day, pencils and notebooks were issued to each prisoner. We went to school that day. The sick and wounded got their schooling at the regimental hospital, a third of a mile away. For obvious reasons, I refused to stay at the hospital. In school we were ordered to take notes. The instructor sounded like an educated man and seemed to know his stuff. He must have been the cream of the crop of English speaking instructors from China. There were platoon instructors under him situated at different locations of the outdoor classroom.

On rainy days, classes were held indoors. The Chinese Reds used different tactics on us. They were very polite, treated us well and tried to brainwash us to become commies. It was so obvious! As far as I can remember, the first subjects were Socialism and Communism. I can remember the instructor saying socialism is the trend today with communism as the final goal. He said Russia is the closest to that goal. I also remember him saying Russia is not yet truly communistic.

After two hours of classes each day, a required one hour discussion period among prisoners was held in our squad rooms. Each group was left alone but we had to be careful because the platoon instructors came around to check on us. We never discussed what we were taught during that one hour period. We just sat around and "talked story." When the platoon instructor came around, we made believe we were discussing things we learned.

At the end of two months, the instructors collected our notebooks and inspected them. I remember some of the boys were called in for not putting more effort at note taking. Our instructors got tired of our lack of interest and classes became less frequent. Gradually classes stopped.

Daily Fare And Life Under our Chinese Captors

Under the Chinese, the food was better. We had all the rice we wanted, no millet or sorghum. They fed us more pork and vegetables. A detail was assigned to go to the regimental headquarters, a third of a mile away, to draw rations for the day.

During the winters of 1951 and 1952, there was little variety in our food because we couldn't get vegetables. In the winter of 1951, we only had turnip soup with rice at each meal. In the winter of 1952, it was potato soup with rice. Sometimes the soup was flavored with some seaweed and sometimes there was some pork in it. We cooked our own food but unlike Monpo, one prisoner from each squad room would bring back the chow for his buddies. We only ate in our rooms. I don't know why.

Ever since we were turned over to the Chinese, they were somewhat lenient about how we used our free time. Some of the prisoners got together and began planning menus from the food available to us. However, every Sunday was sanitation day. We also cleaned our rooms for inspection.

On the matted mud floor, we laid out our blankets with the overcoat over it. At night we slept on it and used comforters as covers. Getting together for bull sessions was also permitted. It was there that I heard for the first time about Major General William Dean, the commander of our division. He had escorted one convoy out of Taejon and had come back for another when he was captured.

The wood cutting detail was the biggest task, especially during the fall. We would go into the forest with armed guards to pick up fallen limbs. We then cut them to size so that we could carry them. We had to store enough wood for cooking and heating our rooms to last us through the winter.

In the winter, many boys from the mainland slept in their cotton padded clothes. I slept only in my underclothing. Strangely, we Hawaii boys took the cold very well. The stove and heater were in the kitchen. As I mentioned before, tunnels ran under the mud floors of the hut to heat the rooms. We were allowed to burn wood for heating or for hot water only two hours a day—from 0600 to 0800 hours in the morning. The floor became hot and usually enough heat was left to last through the night.

The river bank was part of the prison compound. During the summer months, you bathed and washed your clothes when it was convenient to do so. In the two hours we were allowed to heat water, you had to bathe or wash your clothes. During the summer, I got used to being clean because I bathed more often. So during the last winter, I took a bath twice a week.

How cold does it get during the winter nights? At night, if you kept water in a tin cup, the next morning, the water would be frozen solid. There would even be ice around the corners of the room. Mind you, this is where we slept.

Going Home?

On the morning of 11 April, 1953, while I was heating water to take a bath, a guard came into the kitchen and ordered me to pack up. "You are going to the hospital," he said. I didn't know what was going on, my arm was not infected, nor was I sick. I hated to go to the hospital but I had no choice. Fourteen of us were taken to the hospital. We were confined for four days and still did not know what was going on.

One day there was a rumor that the fourteen of us were going home. I had been disappointed too many times and would not believe it. I believed they were sending us to Paekton where a big hospital was located.

On the fifth day, we were taken to a farewell party. We were served sake, fried meat, vegetables and bread. We were also given candy and cigarettes. The Chinese regimental commander was there. He wore no insignia and I couldn't tell what his rank was. He told us that there would be an exchange of sick and wounded prisoners. We were asked what was taken from us when we were first captured. I told them I had $140.00 and a Russian wrist watch taken from me. And would you believe it, they gave me $140.00 and a Russian wrist watch. That convinced me that we were going home.

"You are going home," the Chinese captors said, "and don't forget to fight for peace."

"Sure," I told myself, "we'll fight for China piece by piece, until we free China from your control."

I really had mixed feelings about going home. I was glad to be going home, but was sad, knowing that the others had to stay back and didn't know when they would be repatriated.

"Little Switch" And Finally Home

We were taken to Paekton, the assembly point for all wounded prisoners, and I didn't have a chance to say farewell to my buddies. We left Paekton at 0500 hours on 17 April, 1953, in a 20-ton truck convoy with about 80 prisoners. The trucks were marked with a red flag in the back and a red cloth over the hood. The next day we reached Pyongyang and I couldn't even recognize the city. It was practically flattened by bombs and few buildings were left standing. I don't recall what we did the two days in Pyongyang, but we left that city at 0500 in the morning On 19 April, 1953. The convoy got into Kaesong two days later and we remained in this town for two or three days. Then came the final ride to Panmunjon.

To all those people who get a thrill burning and stomping the American flag, if only they knew what it stood for. I wish they were there with us, when we got off the trucks and started walking across the freedom bridge. When we saw the American flag, waving in the wind, we were so proud. As they say in Hawaii, we got "chicken skin." With tears rolling down our cheeks and our heads held high, we were walking to freedom at last.

From Panmunjon, we were rushed to the 8th Army camp where we were issued new uniforms and met the press. I was given a "Camel" cigarette, although it wasn't my brand. It tasted good after 33 months of the "makeshift" tobacco we were smoking. Next came a cup of coffee, glass of milk, a milk shake, and a stick of chewing gum. These things reminded me of another life. It seemed so unreal, yet, it was real. I was in a daze and couldn't think—33 months and sixteen days as a POW.

A short while later, I went to a holy communion service conducted by an Episcopal chaplain. I felt much better after communion. A helicopter took us to a hospital at Yongdongpo, where we stayed overnight. The next day, a Globemaster flew us to Tokyo and we were transferred to Tokyo General Hospital. We stayed there for

Sus Shinagawa today (Photo Courtesy of Mr. Shinagawa)

three to four days.

Finally, on 1 May, 1953, we boarded a Globemaster and headed for Hawaii. It was a long flight so we had to refuel at Midway Island. The next stop, Hawaii. We flew over the island of Kauai, "my island," the Garden Island, and I could see my hometown from the air. It seemed unreal, for my mind would wander and I could still see the boys at Chongsong prison camp. I could see the things they were doing. The river was just thawing when I left. That meant that winter was gone and "wood details" were coming up. It almost seemed unfair that they remained and I am back in safety. They are going about their hopeless daily routine in the dump, surrounded by hills on every side.

We finally reached Oahu on 1 May, and landed at Hickam Air Force Base. I was surprised to see the crowd. A steward came to me and said that since I was from Hawaii I would be the first off the plane. Someone told me to stop at the top of the ramp, wave to the crowd, than walk slowly down the ramp. I don't remember if I did that or not. Nearby was a parked bus. I entered through the rear door, walked to the front and when I looked out, there to my surprise, the first person I saw was my mom. With tears of joy streaming down my face, I ran to her and hugged her with all my might. She kept rubbing my right arm. I didn't know why. I found out later why she did that. Someone told my family that I had a wounded right arm. My mom and the rest of the family thought that I had lost the arm.

After the surprise welcome and happy reunion with family and friends, all of the repatriates boarded the bus to Tripler General Hospital. I stayed at the hospital for three months and the wound that I received in July 1950 finally healed after a penicillin shot.

I came home with "Little Switch," which was the repatriation of the first group of sick and wounded American POWs from Korea. The rest of the guys came home with "Big Switch" three months later.[4, 5]

Notes

1. In May - June, 1998, the author went to Seoul, Korea. With the aid of Eighth U.S. Army's Korea map experts, he located and verified

all except one of the sites that Sus Shinagawa spent time in as a POW. That exception was Wonson. Wonson is a nonentity. But in its presumed vicinity is Anson. Sus Shinagawa concurs that the city is Anson—he, apparently, misheard it as "Wonson."

2. A foremost expert concerning Korean War POWs is Dr. William Maier, who as a Colonel in the U.S. Army Medical Corps, interviewed 7,000 returning Korean War POWs and veterans. He indicated that hundreds of the emaciated, cold, depressed and forlorn POWs simply gave up all hope and wasted away or died quietly on their bunks or shadowed corner of the room.

3. The Xu Xi (Pin Yin style), according to Dr. Maier and other Chinese Communist indoctrination experts, particularly, psychiatrist Dr. Robert Lifton, divides the six month's course of thought reform into three phases: 1) group identification, a period of togetherness and considerable freedom and enthusiasm; 2) Induced emotional conflict within each individual; 3) Submission and rebirth. When the indoctrination was conducted by a specialist or master the results in converting "weaker" prisoners from their American psyche to one of acceptance of the Chinese inspired thought and political control was remarkable. See John King Fairbank's, *The United States and China,* pp. 292-298 for an excellent discourse on the method.

4. A book written by Fr. Philip Crosbie that parallels Shinagawa's experiences is *March 'Till They Die* (Westminster, MD: Neuman Press, 1956).

5. Susumu "Sus" Shinagawa is now enjoying retirement in his native Hawaii after being employed by the U.S. Army in a civilian capacity for many years.

CHAPTER TWELVE

RACIAL AND ETHNIC RELATIONS IN JAPAN FOLLOWING WORLD WAR II

Introduction

As a Nisei myself, I am keenly interested in how Nihonjin (Japanese) view us, their Nisei or overseas brethren, as well as other ethnic categories who visit, live and work in Japan. This final essay reflects the observations of the author with regard to these subjects, gained while teaching at Minnesota State University, Akita, in 1991. My observations were further elaborated upon in interviews with Japanese students at Century Community College, Japanese visitors and tourists and the Shin-Issei (past WWII immigrants, war brides, as well as recent Japanese brides, and business personnel temporarily located in America)

How the Japanese View their Overseas Brethren

Professor Sarutani of Tokyo Women's College, teaching over Akita's educational channel, presented a fascinating historical discourse on the Issei (first generation emigrants), Nisei (second generation), Sansei (third generation), and Yonsei (fourth generation), Gosei (fifth generation) and even used the generic term "Nikkeijin" (those who trace their ancestry and cultural heritage to Japan). He supported his lecture accurately, going back to the time of Nakahama Manjiro (1840's and 1850's), the Gannen Mono of Hawaii (1867), Okei and the ill-fated Wakamatsu Silk and Tea Colony near Sacramento (1869), and the emigration of Japanese to Latin America, which began in the 1880's. The major points made by Professor Sarutani were:

- Japanese were in the various countries early, within the first 50 to 75 years of the countries' birth.

- The Issei had great difficulties assimilating but they persevered and continued their culture, language, customs, philosophy, religious beliefs and hard work.

- Niseis, for the most part, were nurtured in their parents' beliefs and teachings but, also, entered the new country's culture and daily life through the schools and the country's language.

- Sansei, Yonsei, Gosei and the interracial children—be they 50%, 25%, 12.5% ethnic Japanese, are called "Nikkeijin." Nikkei are unable to speak Japanese fluently and are only vaguely familiar with Japanese customs, attitudes, patterns of thought and their Japanese heritage. Nikkeis are in reality, citizens and people of their birth country.

- Japanese who have emigrated to other countries have contributed greatly to their host countries, examples being Peruvian President Alberto Fujimori, U.S. Senator Daniel Inouye, U.S. Congressman Robert Matsui, former Congressman Norman Mineta, Congresswoman Patsy Mink, deceased Astronaut Colonel Ellison Onizuka, and retired Denver Journalist Bill Hosokawa.

Professor Sarutani then emphasized and reminded his audience that today, Japanese go all over the world and are graciously and respectfully welcomed because their overseas brethren paved the way with hard work, perseverence, and successful accomplishments. He ended his remarks by urging all Japanese to become knowledgeable about their foreign cousins, the Nikkei.

Recently, many newspaper and magazine articles as well as TV programs, have featured the Nikkei. Over 70,000 have gone to Japan to seek their fortunes. They are from Brazil, Peru, Argentina, Mexico, and Bolivia. Japanese nationals favor them as workers because they are Japanese in name, appearance, and general behavior. Yet, they are "unJapanese" because they cannot speak, read or write Japanese. So, communication is a problem and, at times, custom and tradition may not be followed by the Nikkei. This has been a concern for some employers. But they are hard workers and they do the boring, repetitive type of factory and manufacture work that do not appeal to the Japanese. In Japan, they are able to earn enough to return to Latin America within six months, for vacations, and to send home monthly remittances that provide the financial support for their families.

Other Minorities in Japan

Japanese employers and the government favor the Nikkei workers because of the blood ties—they are ethnic Japanese and so the homogeneity of the nation and its peoples is not threatened. This thinking is in deep contrast to attitudes toward other foreign workers in Japan. They, especially those from the third world countries like Bangladesh, Iran and Pakistan, face discrimination in jobs, housing, and general social acceptance. Southeast Asians like the Filipinos, Thais, Cambodians, and Malayans are looked upon as "lesser Asians" and not in the same league as the Japanese and they are relegated to the servile or even menial kinds of work.

Koreans are in a different "anxiety" category for the Japanese and their government. Historically, Japan's ambitions concerning Korea go back to the 1590's when Toyotomi Hideyoshi invaded Korea. Also, the Russo-Japanese War of 1904-05 brought Korea into Japan's orbit of influence and Japan formally annexed Korea in 1910. Ironically, Korea was the pipeline through which the magnificent cultural attainments of China flowed to Japan. Korean artisans and religions came to Japan and introduced the best of their pottery making, scroll painting and Buddhist and Confucian religion and philosophies.

Before and during WWII, Koreans were forcibly drafted and made to work in Japan's coal mines or heavy steel and shipbuilding plants. A tragic saga of the WWII treatment of Koreans is now being reflected in the reparations appeal and brutality charges made by the wartime "comfort-women" against the Japanese government.

Discrimination continues to plague the Koreans. At present there are 790,000 Koreans, many who are third and fourth generation Koreans, living in Japan. Japan has steadfastly denied them full benefits that Japanese citizens enjoy. They are considered aliens and until recently were fingerprinted annually.

Koreans in Japan are proud of being Korean and show their nationalism by wearing their colorful national dresses and by loudly agitating for their rights as permanent residents. They keep up their heritage through language schools, civic and patriotic organizations, be they supporters of North or South Korea. Also, since Japanese are imbued with the *enryo* (be humble, be non-aggressive, be non-pushy) trait, the Koreans are looked upon as being too loud and too aggressive. Some Japanese have even accused Koreans of being involved with underworld activities. To this day Japanese tend to look down upon and discriminate against the Koreans. Now with the rise of modern Korea's economy, Japan is becoming more concerned with Korea's competitive nature and industrial advancements.

Chinese (to include the Taiwanese) in Japan are generally looked upon favorably as representing the best of ancient China's magnificent civilization. The Japanese perception is influenced by the future world power status of a gargantuan China and, also,

Chinese cuisine is thoroughly enjoyed by the Japanese. In general, Chinese do not face the snide remarks that may be uttered against Koreans or other third world foreigners.

Caucasians, especially those with fair skin, light colored eyes and hair (Anglos) are the "cream" of foreigners as far as Japanese acceptance is concerned. True, they do face the annoying stares and quips of "*Gaijin da, Gaijin da*" (foreigner) but that is more a nuisance to be overcome rather than outright discrimination. Marriage to Caucasians is no longer looked upon as a rarity or oddity.

Blacks are discriminated against, too, but not in the same vein as third worlders. Blacks are pictured as enviable athletes and jazz musicians so it is not a case of outright fear, bitterness, and scorn. The Japanese respect and admire blacks for their abilities, and those Japanese youth who are aware of the latest in avant-garde music show tremendous enthusiasm for black music and musicians. Jazz and rock concerts are perennially sold out and video shops do a high volume of sales on videos, tapes, CDs and boom boxes that feature black musicians.

Japanese, early on, learn that their homogeneity makes them unique and perhaps this is why others feel slighted, discriminated against and different. Japanese strict attention to order, discipline, one's place in society and being Japanese is best explained in the terms "*uchi*" and "*soto.*" The Japanese consider themselves as uchi—inner, the house—and all others are soto, outside. So non-Japanese are outsiders, the "gaijin" or foreigners. Insiders are privy to everything Japanese and outsiders are treated differently. As Professor John C. Condon noted in his book *Wtih Respect to the Japanese*, "Japanese make a much clearer distinction between what pertains to the family, or school group or company (the "house") and matters that are outside of those domains."

References

Condon, John C.,*With Respect To The Japanese* (Yarmouth, ME: Intercultural Press, Inc., 1984).

ABOUT THE AUTHOR: Historian Edwin M. Nakasone is a University of Minnesota graduate and a long time member of the history faculty of Century College, White Bear Lake, Minnesota. Born and raised in Hawaii, he witnessed the attack on Pearl Harbor, Wheeler Army Airfield, and Schofield Barracks on December 7, 1941. He served in the United States Army as an interpreter during the Occupation of Japan in 1947-1948. He is a retired colonel, United  States Army. Professor Nakasone teaches World War II history, Asian history and Asian Pacific American history. He has travelled widely, authored many papers, several books, and produced several videos on WWII. He was the recipient of two Fulbright grants, one to Japan in 1965 and the other to India in 1981. His popular "Pearl Harbor Remembered" dramatization has been widely acclaimed and has been presented to hundreds of schools, colleges, clubs, military and veteran's groups, community service clubs, chambers of commerce and history organizations.